W9-AQT-695

Improving
Government
Performance

John J. DiIulio, Jr.
Gerald Garvey
Donald F. Kettl

Improving Government Performance

An Owner's Manual

CARNEGIE LIBRARY
LIVINGSTONE COLLEGE
SALISBURY, NC 28144

The Brookings Institution
Washington, D.C.

125140

Copyright © 1993 by
THE BROOKINGS INSTITUTION
1775 Massachusetts Avenue, N.W., Washington, D.C. 20036

All rights reserved

Library of Congress Catalogue Card Number 93-079264
ISBN 0-8157-1855-1

9 8 7 6 5 4 3 2 1

The paper used in this publication meets the minimum requirements of
the American National Standard for Information Sciences—Perma-
nence of Paper for Printed Library Materials, ANSI Z39.48-1984

Ⓑ THE BROOKINGS INSTITUTION

The Brookings Institution is an independent organization devoted to nonpartisan research, education, and publication in economics, government, foreign policy, and the social sciences generally. Its principal purposes are to aid in the development of sound public policies and to promote public understanding of issues of national importance.

The Institution was founded on December 8, 1927, to merge the activities of the Institute for Government Research, founded in 1916, the Institute of Economics, founded in 1922, and the Robert Brookings Graduate School of Economics and Government, founded in 1924.

The Board of Trustees is responsible for the general administration of the Institution, while the immediate direction of the policies, program, and staff is vested in the President, assisted by an advisory committee of the officers and staff. The by-laws of the Institution state: "It is the function of the Trustees to make possible the conduct of scientific research, and publication, under the most favorable conditions, and to safeguard the independence of the research staff in the pursuit of their studies and in the publication of the results of such studies. It is not a part of their function to determine, control, or influence the conduct of particular investigations or the conclusions reached."

The President bears final responsibility for the decision to publish a manuscript as a Brookings book. In reaching his judgment on the competence, accuracy, and objectivity of each study, the President is advised by the director of the appropriate research program and weighs the views of a panel of expert outside readers who report to him in confidence on the quality of the work. Publication of a work signifies that it is deemed a competent treatment worthy of public consideration but does not imply endorsement of conclusions or recommendations.

The Institution maintains its position of neutrality on issues of public policy in order to safeguard the intellectual freedom of the staff. Hence interpretations or conclusions in Brookings publications should be understood to be solely those of the authors and should not be attributed to the Institution, to its trustees, officers, or other staff members, or to the organizations that support its research.

Board of Trustees

John C. Whitehead
Chairman

Leonard Abramson
Ronald J. Arnault
Elizabeth E. Bailey
Rex J. Bates
A. W. Clausen
John L. Clendenin
Kenneth W. Dam
D. Ronald Daniel
Walter Y. Elisha

Stephen Friedman
William H. Gray, III
Teresa Heinz
F. Warren Hellman
Samuel Hellman
James A. Johnson
Thomas W. Jones
Vernon E. Jordan, Jr.
James A. Joseph
Nannerl O. Keohane
Martin J. Koldyke

Thomas G. Labrecque
Donald F. McHenry
Bruce K. MacLaury
Constance Berry Newman
Maconda Brown O'Connor
Samuel Pisar
David Rockefeller, Jr.
Howard D. Samuel
Ralph S. Saul
Robert H. Smith
John D. Zeglis
Ezra K. Zilkha

Honorary Trustees

Vincent M. Barnett, Jr.
Barton M. Biggs
Louis W. Cabot
Edward W. Carter
Frank T. Cary
William T. Coleman, Jr.
Lloyd N. Cutler
Bruce B. Dayton
Douglas Dillon
Charles W. Duncan, Jr.
Robert F. Erburu

Robert D. Haas
Huntington Harris
Andrew Heiskell
Roger W. Heyns
Roy M. Huffington
John E. Lockwood
James T. Lynn
William McC. Martin, Jr.
Robert S. McNamara
Mary Patterson McPherson
Arjay Miller

Donald S. Perkins
J. Woodward Redmond
Charles W. Robinson
James D. Robinson III
Robert V. Roosa
B. Francis Saul II
Henry B. Schacht
Gerard C. Smith
Robert Brookings Smith
Morris Tanenbaum
James D. Wolfensohn

Foreword

PUBLIC SERVICE REFORM is once again on the agenda of a new administration. President Clinton has commissioned, and Vice President Gore is directing, a National Performance Review, an ambitious undertaking designed to make the federal government work better and cost less. Inspired by David Osborne and Ted Gaebler's best-selling book, *Reinventing Government*, the NPR is working feverishly to produce a blueprint for a refurbished, entrepreneurial, customer-driven federal bureaucracy.

This volume provides a historical and theoretical overview of efforts to reform the federal bureaucracy. Drawing on scholarly research, the authors offer lessons and prescriptions that are both practical and timely. They argue that "evolution" is a more appropriate metaphor for improving government performance than "reinvention," and that constructive change is more likely to occur experimentally and gradually than as an attempted sweeping transformation of the public sector.

John J. DiIulio, Jr., is professor of politics and public affairs at Princeton University and nonresident senior fellow at Brookings; Gerald Garvey is professor of politics at Princeton; and Donald F. Kettl is professor of political science and public affairs at the University of Wisconsin, Madison.

The authors would like to thank Christopher Foreman, Constance Horner, Thomas Mann, Richard Neustadt, Bert Rockman, and Allen Schick for their timely and constructive comments on a draft of the manuscript. The authors would also like to thank Jim Schneider for editing the manuscript, Alison Rimsky for verifying it, Cindy Terrels for assistance with word processing, Susan Woollen for typesetting the manuscript, and Michael Treadway for compiling the index.

The views expressed in this book are those of the authors and should not be ascribed to the persons whose assistance is acknowledged, or to the trustees, officers, or other staff members of the Brookings Institution.

Bruce K. MacLaury
President

July 1993
Washington, D.C.

Contents

ix

Introduction

Two Metaphors of Reform—Invention and Evolution

FROM THE BEGINNING, two metaphors of reform have vied for primacy in the American imagination. The first, the metaphor of invention, came out of the founders' own preoccupation with Newtonian mechanism. They thought it possible to create a self-checking governmental apparatus, a "machine that would go of itself." Thomas Jefferson urged that the structures of government be abolished and reinvented every twentieth Independence Day. When William Gladstone described the U.S. Constitution as "the greatest work ever struck off by the mind and wit of man," he was invoking the imagery of institutional invention, as was James Bryce when he wrote admiringly of our political system as the "federal contrivance."

In a nation of gadgetmakers and tinkerers, Eli Whitney, Thomas Edison, and Henry Ford have become folk icons. It is natural to identify constructive change with the act of invention, and probably just as natural to suppose that some reinventing may be in order when institutional change seems needed. Much of the appeal today of David Osborne's and Ted Gaebler's *Reinventing Government* derives from the resonance of their main metaphor with American political culture.[1] They write of catalytic government. Their "map," as they term it, for a New World of governance is itself a catalytic image, intended as much to galvanize

1

action as to describe reality. Similarly, the metaphor of invention, which gives their book its thematic unity and resonance, serves more a catalytic than an analytic purpose. The can-do spirit, change effected through ingenious new combinations of parts, reform as the product of a single creative event—these are among the ideas evoked by our self-conception as an inventive people.

The other metaphor, the metaphor of evolution, has as much intellectual support as does the metaphor of invention. If our Constitution was invented, it was also left open and adaptable, the better to accommodate developments that "could not have been foreseen completely by the most gifted of its begetters," as Justice Oliver Wendell Holmes commented. The doctrine of social Darwinism no longer commands the kind of assent it once did. But the thoroughness with which Americans embraced the evolutionary paradigm when it first appeared suggests that gradualists such as Charles Darwin, Herbert Spencer, and Alfred Marshall, though Britons themselves, expounded a truth that citizens of the United States accept almost instinctively.

One of the basic concepts of contemporary social science, that of bounded rationality, supports the evolutionary approach to institutional reform. According to the bounded rationality hypothesis, policymakers mostly delude themselves when they think that "comprehensive study" or "bold inventive action" can produce useful, enduring change. The world of politics is too rich in both information and uncertainty; once-and-for-all efforts at structural reform must fail. When used as an evocative symbol, the metaphor of invention can help concentrate the mind, charge the imagination, perhaps inspire a certain willing suspension of disbelief. But the inventive approach has its limits as a guide to practical action. The elements of public management cannot be detached from their political and institutional contexts in ways that would permit them to be manipulated inventively.

We are limited in the administrative knowledge that we already possess. We are still struggling to process information about the Old World of governance, let alone about anyone's imagined map for a New World. The primary teaching of modern implementation scholars is that projects for institutional reform may produce unintended consequences, frequently unwanted ones. This literature itself grew out of efforts to understand why the attempts at reinvention of American society in the 1960s had failed.

History and social theory alike suggest that the optimism of the reinventors, although necessary to concentrate energies, will best help improve government performance if it is tempered with caution. The evolutionary approach does not deny the richness or the value of the proposals Osborne and Gaebler offer. From one end of their book to the other, the good ideas just keep coming. Moreover, they have generated reform energy unmatched in a generation. Constructive change, however, is more likely to occur selectively and experimentally than as a sweeping transformation of the public sector.

Reformers need periodically to recall that incremental, experimental change has usually proved to be the way institutional reforms become simultaneously feasible, constructive, and enduring. We intend this book as a brief for a reformist attitude that is careful, prudent, and experimental—one that will work, and one that will last.

1

Thinking Beyond the Rhetoric of Reform

THE PAST FEW YEARS have been a time of renewed interest in public service reform at all levels of government. In 1990 the National Commission on the Public Service, chaired by former Federal Reserve Board Chairman Paul A. Volcker, issued its report, which focused on the federal service.[2] In 1993 the National Commission on the State and Local Public Service, chaired by former Mississippi Governor William F. Winter, presented its report to President Clinton. Now comes the National Performance Review, commissioned by President Clinton, directed by Vice President Gore, and largely inspired by *Reinventing Government*, perhaps the first public administration book in history to become a bestseller.

Much of the allure of this book, written by journalist David Osborne and former city manager Ted Gaebler, derives from its diagnosis of the causes of inadequate federal performance and its energetic prescriptions for change. The diagnosis: a bureaucracy staffed by well-meaning officials who find themselves hamstrung by illogical procedures and pulled in unproductive directions by perverse incentives. The prescription: decentralize government and create incentives to promote entrepreneurial activity by government workers.

Reinventing Government reminded everyone that government is after all in business to serve citizens, not its own employees (whether elective or appointive). The book established the critical importance of a good working relationship between government and the private sector. Perhaps most important, it raised the debate on the quality of government performance to a level not seen in a generation.

The National Performance Review

The National Performance Review, sometimes called the "reinventing government initiative," takes much of its agenda, as well as its informal title, from Osborne's and Gaebler's book. Vice President Gore outlined the goals of the review at a press conference on April 15, 1993: evaluate the efficiency of every federal agency, identify and eliminate waste and inefficiency throughout the federal service, streamline the federal personnel system, and change the culture of federal bureaucracy and "empower" workers. Some 200 federal employees have become the eyes, ears, hands, and feet of the National Performance Review. They are organized into various reinvention teams. Together they are to gather detailed data and fashion prescriptive analyses on the performance of all federal agencies, addressing themselves in particular to the efficacy of various leadership strategies and management structures. And they are to do all this by Labor Day 1993, at which time the vice president has promised to unveil the Clinton administration's blueprint for a reinvented government.

The effort rests on broad public opinion that it is indeed past time to rethink the balance of public and private sector responsibilities. It is time to rearrange the organization of the federal bureaucracy in a way that will shorten internal lines of communication and promote coordination across functional and jurisdictional boundaries. It is time to decentralize government so as to facilitiate entrepreneurial activity by civil servants and ultimately change the culture of public bureaucracy.

The results of the 1992 presidential election emphasized the American public's expectation of constructive change. And even a cursory examination of federal management practices demonstrates why this expectation rises to the level of a demand. No one, however, should underestimate how hard it will be to change patterns of bureaucratic operation, organizational forms, and structural constraints that have evolved over the course of a century. Short-term confidence and enthusiasm are obvious requirements. The competence and dedication of federal administrators working without fanfare and often without thanks represent even higher values. One hopes that, fifteen years from now, GS-11s throughout the federal government will be daily serving the public even more effectively than is now the case, for reasons that can be traced back to reforms identified by the national performance reviewers. To this end, it is crucial that the energetic officials in the White House and Congress who are spearheading reform efforts not become so captivated by the rhetoric of reform that they look past the realities.

In truth, the federal government as it functions today cannot be reinvented because it was not invented in the first place. The bureaucracy evolved through pragmatic, almost catch-as-catch-can responses to particular problems as they appeared. It is this development that warns of the need for an incremental, evolutionary, experimental approach to institutional reform.

An Incremental, Evolutionary, Experimental Process

The evolutionary viewpoint carries implications about the sources of problems in the federal bureaucracy. It implies as well the responses that will work best as public managers begin trying to alter a process that has evolved over generations. The history of federal reform efforts counsels humility, not hubris.

Contrary to what President Clinton said when he announced

the reform initiative, past public service reports have not simply gathered dust. The 1993 National Performance Review is only the most recent presidential effort to make government work better (figure 1). In 1912 President Taft's Commission on Economy and Efficiency argued for a presidential budget based on performance. In 1937 the Brownlow committee concluded that "the president needs help" and argued for a strengthened executive management capacity emanating from the White House. Members of two post–World War II commissions headed by former President Hoover studied every organizational aspect of the federal government. President Kennedy's budget director headed a task force on problems in government contracting, and President Johnson's task force on government organization examined ways to improve the president's management of it. The Nixon administration followed with a high-powered advisory council headed by industrialist Roy Ash to recommend changes in executive organization. Under Ronald Reagan, yet another blue ribbon panel studied the problems of federal acquisition, focusing on the Defense Department, and in 1983 a commission headed by J. Peter Grace claimed to have found hundreds of billions of dollars of waste in federal programs.

Some Lessons—and Some Temptations

Four important lessons emerge from these attempts at reform. First, the task of institutional reform is daunting. If solutions were easy, repeated efforts would not have been necessary. Second, despite the difficulty of the job, progress, albeit gradual, partial, and selective, has been made. Government works better today because of these earlier reform efforts. Neither the Brownlow committee nor the Hoover commissions caused the earth to move, but they did cause government to improve, although selectively and incrementally. The Brownlow committee strengthened the institutional presidency; the Hoover commissions

Figure 1. Major Commissions to Improve the Executive Branch, 1905–93

Keep commission (1905–09)
Personnel management, government contracting, information management

President's Commission on Economy and Efficiency (1910–13)
The case for a national executive budget

Joint Committee on Reorganization (1921–24)
Methods of redistributing executive functions among the departments

President's Committee on Administrative Management (1936–37)
Recommended creation of the Executive Office of the President; study founded on substantial academic theory

First Hoover commission (1947–49)
Comprehensive review of the organization and function of the executive branch; built on task force reports

Second Hoover commission (1953–55)
Follow-on to the first Hoover commission; focused more on policy problems than organizational structure

Study commissions on executive reorganization (1953–68)
Series of low-key reforms that produced quiet but important changes

Ash council (1969–71)
Proposals for a fundamental restructuring of the executive branch, including creation of four new super departments to encompass existing departments

Carter reorganization effort (1977–79)
Bottom-up, process-based effort to reorganize government that mostly ended in failure; new cabinet departments created independently of effort

Grace commission (1982–84)
Large-scale effort to determine how government could be operated for less money

National Performance Review (1993)
Attempt to "reinvent" government to improve its performance

Source: Ronald C. Moe, *Reorganizing the Executive Branch in the Twentieth Century: Landmark Commissions*, report 92-293 GOV (Congressional Research Service, March 1992).

launched management reforms that revolutionized the government's day-to-day business. Third, reforms have worked best when they grew from a strong strategy and robust intellectual support. Performance reviews are, in their essence, efforts at strategic planning. They themselves need to be guided by a strategic plan, a clear vision of the problem and of the direction in which solutions lie. In fact, diagnosing the problem has always been the most critical step in every reform effort. The Brownlow committee's famous finding, "the president needs help," fueled its work and helped ensure its success. Fourth, long-term follow-through matters. Only sustained presidential attention to management problems will produce a difference.

The record also suggests four temptations that today's reformers must avoid. First, it is tempting to confuse disagreement over what government ought to do with how well it does it. There is a common presumption that government programs are larded with too much bureaucracy and wasteful spending. But what critics call waste, fraud, and abuse often are programs managed well but managed according to values different from the critics' own. Many of the potential savings identified by the Grace commission, for example, would have resulted from eliminating programs with which commission members disagreed. The programs might indeed have been wasteful by some definitions, but they represented the legitimate product of the American democratic process. The danger here is that solutions billed as administrative, managerial, or technical may disguise underlying differences of policy or significant competition among disparate interests. No one should be surprised when the promised results are not achieved: the proponents of the changes have underestimated the political strength of forces that would resist change.

A second temptation to avoid is not only rushing to judgment but rushing into action. Reformers need to examine closely the problems they wish to solve and assess carefully the actions required to solve them. Some kinds of reforms require major changes in legislation; others can be effectively pursued through executive action. Legislative changes require not only more time but also more elaborate political strategies to implement. Administrative changes can sometimes be done more rapidly. Reforms must be staged according to the strategies required to implement them.

Poor implementation can doom any policy. Proceeding in a do-it-all-now manner, without matching the political resources required and the objectives sought, is likely to stall a reform effort. Easy changes that might have been completed at low cost may be left undone because energy goes into difficult long-term projects. These long-term projects might better be approached by steadily applying pressure over time while building on the political impetus that beginning the easier jobs can generate. The trick is to do what can be done quickly by administrative means while preparing a legislative agenda for the long term.

Third, it is tempting to promise that management reforms will produce major savings and reduce the budget deficit. Improved performance is in fact likely to produce budget savings, but only as a by-product. Some improvements in performance might yield greater satisfaction with government services without making much difference on the bottom line. New procedures for processing social security checks, for example, might dramatically decrease the number of lost checks without reducing the deficit. Other improvements might require short-term investments in exchange for significant long-term savings. Many government contracts, for instance, are plagued by mismanagement. Reducing such problems requires investing in greater government expertise to ensure that the public gets its money's worth in the long run. In most systems, optimum performance requires balancing costs against quality. Making cost savings the driving force of a performance review can detract from quality. And mingling management issues with budget questions typically increases the suspicion of government employees who have seen previous performance reforms degenerate into witch hunts to cut their salaries and criticize their work. The performance review process itself has to be a model of the values it seeks to instill more widely within government.

There is an important connection between government performance and the budget. Regardless of the policy changes that might occur, the federal government will continue to manage a great many functions, from space exploration and energy conservation to income security and environmental regulation. The government must get its money's worth. Good management can keep costs down and improve results; poor management will drive costs up, yield diminished results, and increase the budget deficit. Improved government performance thus supports the drive for deficit reduction, but the two are not synonymous.

Finally, it is tempting for study commissions to seek The Answer. But implementation scholars and leaders in the total quality management (TQM) movement have emphasized continuous improvement, incremental, evolutionary, experimental improvement. Reconstructing government will require carefully paced modifications informed by an experimental rather than a dogmatic or recklessly inventive spirit.

Not even the most prescient reformers can know what will work best. Studying today's government performance problems can provide a starting place but rarely a realistic picture of the ending place. By contrast, with a process that everyone expects to be evolutionary, careful reviews of interim results can provide real guidance on what works and why. Trying, evaluating, and learning through time are as important for ultimate success as the original study design.

No one who has thought seriously about leadership and management will presume to know what works best under all conditions. Nor can a clear vision emerge from ideas collected from government workers. Ford Motor Company may have been dramatically improved the quality of its cars by acting on the suggestions of assembly line workers. But it could never use such suggestions to decide what kind of car to build. Thought without action is futile; but action without thought directed by a clear strategy can be fatal. Our first purpose is therefore to understand the sources and nature of both the structures and the bureaucratic culture that, so many Americans are convinced, prevent public officials from performing with initiative and imagination.

2

The Evolution of the Federal Bureaucracy

THE PROGRESSIVES established the basic mechanisms of America's modern public administration: new cabinet departments, independent commissions, blueprints for the modern Executive Office of the President, the civil service system, and the presidential budget. Since then, the federal bureaucracy has evolved through agency-by-agency, procedure-by-procedure, program-by-program responses to problems as they appeared. That process has left a vast, untidy apparatus. The historical view gives a useful perspective for understanding today's problems.

A Pattern of Agency-by-Agency Growth

In 1887 Congress created the Interstate Commerce Commission and two years later elevated the commissioner of Agriculture to full cabinet status—this after a century in which the United States had gotten along with the original executive departments plus one (the Interior Department, established in 1849). The Progressive movement launched a bureaucratic evolution that produced in the next century today's complex of independent regulatory commissions, executive agencies, and fourteen executive departments.

Most of the classical theorists of bureaucracy, from

leaders of American progressivism such as Woodrow Wilson and Frederick Winslow Taylor through Max Weber and Luther Gulick, took it more or less for granted that institutional arrangements matter and that a bureaucrat's performance and a bureau's design are interrelated. Central to the classical tradition was that efficiency is the objective of organization and functional specialization is the way to achieve efficiency. As a result, government acquired additional functions, and it became increasingly differentiated and complex as new commissions and agencies proliferated. Specialized bureaus were the institutional response to new problems.

This theory became the blueprint for the exponential growth of government. Americans have always seemed quick to pass a law, create a bureau, issue new rules, and enlarge the bureaucracy when a problem appeared that the market seemed incapable of handling. Government became society's problem solver of last resort.

First the Progressives created the new independent commissions and executive agencies to deal with market failures. The Interstate Commerce Commission (not to mention dozens of ratesetting commissions in the states) coped with natural monopolies in capital-intensive industries. The Federal Reserve Board regulated the supply of money and credit. The Food and Drug Administration protected the public from contaminants in food and pharmaceutical products. Between 1890 and the mid-1920s almost all of the executive departments expanded, as did the apparatus that would become the Executive Office of the President. And in the same years the Commerce and Labor departments were created. When the Great Depression showed that the unregulated private economy can fail to generate full employment, government accepted responsibility for providing economic stimulation and stabilization. The New Deal added the Civilian Conservation Corps (CCC), the Work Projects Administration (WPA), the National Recovery Administration (NRA), and other alphabet agencies.

The additions and expansions continued after World

War II, but with a social rather than an economic focus. The federal government accepted responsibility when troubled social institutions (the family, the neighborhood) failed. Yet another set of programs, from aid to families with dependent children to community development, was created and expanded through yet another set of bureaus established to administer them.

Throughout this bureaucratic growth, many new commissions and agencies reflected existing industries. New programs grew to promote home building or road construction. Other programs, such as the war on poverty or AIDS research, helped stimulate whole new industries. The growth of the federal bureaucracy is thus linked as well with fundamental changes in the private sector. These changes have also created political interests with a huge stake in government activity that have transformed the workings of the American political system.

Functional Specialization and Boundary Problems

The evolution of federal responsibilities explains much of the patchwork pattern of our government. It has created specialized agencies divided by jurisdictional boundaries. These boundaries have multiplied as new agencies and programs have grown, and difficulties of coordination have proliferated in tandem. At the same time, the structure of Congress and the bureaucracy came to mirror one another. Congress often created a new legislative subcommittee to oversee the work of a new commission or agency. The number of congressional subcommittees grew apace with the industry-by-industry growth of the economy and the agency-by-agency growth of the bureaucracy. By this process, some scholars contend, the "iron triangles" of American government first appeared: new bureaus linked by relationships of continuing influence to counterpart legislative subcommittees as well as to the firms in their respective counterpart industries.

CARNEGIE LIBRARY
LIVINGSTONE COLLEGE
SALISBURY, NC 28144

Today, for example, relieving rural poverty requires cooperation among officials from many federal agencies, beginning with the Department of Agriculture and its own subunits (the Rural Electrification Administration and so forth), but including Health and Human Services, Housing and Urban Development, and various subunits of Interior (the Bureau of Indian Affairs, the Bureau of Land Management). In this area alone, substantial energy must go into securing coordination. Across the government as a whole, the energy devoted to cross-boundary competition and coordination detracts in incalculable ways from officials' attention to solving the public's problems.

In the Environmental Protection Agency organizational issues present other problems. Offices are organized and staffed to deal with pollution in specific media (air, water, ground). It is a familiar lament that efforts to correct problems within the jurisdiction of one specialized office create new pollution problems for another: enforced scrubbing of smokestacks to clean smoke plumes of sulfur oxides generates hundreds of thousands of tons of sludge each year that has to be buried in landfills or dumped offshore. As in poverty programs, the structure of government too often gets in the way.

The proliferation of specialized executive bureaus, legislative subcommittees, and private sector interests around these issues has also meant that responsibility for every problem from environmental safety to adequate health care overlaps. Classical organization theory was based on the unity of command. Today, overlapping jurisdictions create endless jockeying for lead-agency status on high-profile problems. Because many agencies have a stake in, but no clear responsibility for, other problems, solutions fall through the cracks. The virtue of organizational specialization has turned into the vice of organizational fragmentation. Incoherence in policymaking and confusion in implementation have resulted.

The irony is that the efforts of the Progressives to improve the rationality and effectiveness of the federal government created the conditions encouraging the fragmentation and overlap we are now struggling to solve. The lessons for reformers are important. Past solutions too often become present problems; seeking today's solutions from yesterday's models can be dangerous.

3

The Contemporary Critique of Bureaucracy

AMONG MOST PROFESSIONAL government watchers, and certainly among other citizens, any enthusiasm that once existed for bureaucracy has dwindled to disillusionment. The typical observer today is more likely to view government (bureaucracy) as the core of the problem and replacing bureaucratic power with market mechanisms as the solution. These mechanisms include transferring more public responsibilities to the private sector, contracting out more of the functions that remain in public hands, increasing competition among public providers of services, and encouraging public managers to behave more entrepreneurially by increasing the incentives for good performance. The reforms have marched under a host of banners, but they share the belief that marketlike competition produces better results than government monopoly power. If the government is to have responsibility for a job, it ought to be subject as much as possible to competitive pressures.

The inadequacies of the Progressive design as it has evolved have produced many new theories to reform bureaucracy. These theories have underscored the importance of four interrelated phenomena: the risk that the exercise of bureaucratic discretion and power will distort the public interest, the efforts of elected officials to seek to control this power, related efforts within the bureaucracy to direct administrative discretion, and the problems of balancing these controls with workers' need for motivation.

The Risks of Bureaucratic Discretion

Grant McConnell, whose *Private Power and American Democracy* many regard as the classic critique of the Progressives' theory, emphasized the tendency of the Progressive Era legislators to use open-ended statutory charters when delegating powers to the experts in the agencies.[3] The legislators assumed that administrators could be trusted because of their ethic of service and professionalism. The typical Progressive regulatory statute contained mandates hardly more specific than "certify new facilities when they are in 'the public convenience and necessity'" or "set 'just and reasonable' rates." The vagueness of these standards inevitably endowed bureaucrats with great discretionary powers. The vagueness also inadvertently encouraged powerful lobbyists to influence agency rules and enforcement policies according to their own ends. The Progressives, in effect, all but invited agency "capture" by private interests. McConnell's interpretation established the iron triangle imagery of a public policy process dominated by self-dealing bureaucrats, congressional committees, and interest groups, with the public interest excluded from deliberations.[4]

These public-private connections have caused intense concern because the opportunities for and the effects of administrative discretion by public officials are today far better understood. Administrative discretion is the base for real administrative power that is hard to control. The large funds of private interests, the number of congressional subcommittees, and the intricacy of policy decisions all make it much easier for policymaking to become dominated by a handful of players.

The iron triangle critique raises serious questions about relying on the private sector to reform public processes. Private competition may provide more incentives for efficiency than public monopoly, but it also increases the danger that private interests will dominate the public policy process. The danger of capture of the public interest by private money is well understood. So too are the virtues of private competition. Far less well understood is how these two ideas collide: how using private competition can increase the odds that private, not public, interests will dominate bureaucrats' decisions.

The Progressives assumed that the civil service reforms of the Pendleton Act (appointment by merit, tenure in service) would ensure accountability in the public service. These values thus laid the foundation for staffing government with experts and improving its efficiency. It has turned out, however, not to be so easy to ensure rectitude and accountability in our public agencies, or at least not without costs that the Progressives did not foresee.

Relationships between public and private sectors that become too cozy obviously threaten the integrity of the administrative process. Because the iron triangle structure creates a natural context for forbidden deal making, a vast network of regulations now controls the behavior of government officials and the private sector representatives with whom they come into frequent contact. Certainly these rules do promote rectitude and accountability. But they do so by compromising morale and efficiency. Kenneth Culp Davis has called the attempt to confine and constrain official behavior "structuring discretion."[5]

To prevent the abuse of bureaucratic discretion, both the president and Congress have struggled to structure discretion. Their efforts, however, have too often shackled administrators and crippled their performance.

Controlling Discretion through Executive and Legislative Means

The externally imposed controls on today's federal bureaucracy begin with elaborate rules written by the Office of Management and Budget. OMB imposes rules on federal paperwork, advance clearance for regulations and congressional testimony, information collection, and financial accounting. Even more important, it reviews agency budgets. Through these mechanisms, OMB exercises powerful control over agency behavior. Managers understandably chafe under the restrictions. They complain that OMB overcontrols, that it does not support administrative flexibility and insists on meaningless central clearance that delays the administrative process and increases costs. Central clearance is important to ensure that agency decisions are consistent with administrative policy, but

OMB needs to better manage its central clearance function to ensure a more productive balance of central policy control and decentralized managerial flexibility.

Improving OMB management, however, cannot in itself restrain the excesses of external bureaucratic controls. The president might be the chief executive, but federal agencies are the creatures of Congress, which creates the programs, authorizes spending, dictates organizational structure, sets personnel ceilings, and enacts crosscutting regulations such as procurement and financial accounting standards. Congress, especially in committee, is also far more interested in detail than the president in overseeing federal agencies. Even OMB does not match congressional committees in the carefulness of program oversight. The closer one looks at the way agencies behave and the problems they produce, the more their behavior seems the product of congressional action. In creating the Superfund program, for example, Congress set a ceiling for the share of the program's funds that could be spent on EPA's own staff—members wanted to ensure that they were not creating an agency that would acquire a permanent life to manage what they considered a temporary program. As a result, EPA has delegated most Superfund operations and many policy decisions to contractors. The program's problems, in turn, have often been the products of an uneasy relationship between EPA and its contractors. But congressional action was the driving force in shaping Superfund's performance.

Divided political control and a culture of micromanagement have also conditioned how Congress approaches administrative agencies. In an era of divided party control of government, federal agencies have been squarely in the cross-hairs of disputes between presidents and members of Congress. How an agency ought to behave, whether it is the military in its policy toward homosexuals or the Food and Drug Administration in its procedures for licensing new drugs, has become the focus of interbranch battles. And even though Congress pays careful attention to what federal agencies do, members have little interest and less capacity to examine management fundamentals. Congressional incentives to claim credit for action have produced a tendency to hunt for instances of waste, fraud, and abuse in policy arenas from housing rehabilitation to defense contracting. That, in turn, has led Congress to focus on narrow administrative details to the exclusion of broad trends.

These three trends—overcontrol by OMB, divided party control of Congress and the executive, and micromanagement by Congress—have created procedural straitjackets that limit the flexibility of managers to solve the problems they encounter. A focus on narrow, sometimes embarrassing details to the exclusion of overall performance has created strong incentives for agency managers to avoid taking risks: small aberrations can quickly attract big political attention. This is not to say that major problems do not deserve careful examination and sharp criticism. But given the way the Congress often treats administrators, there are few incentives and less capacity to determine whether headline-grabbing problems are part of a serious trend or whether even more serious performance problems are slipping by unnoticed because they do not generate horror stories. Congressional hearings into $600 toilet seats grab headlines, even though the price can be explained through admittedly complex and sometimes bizarre government accounting standards. Other programs such as medicare, however, have attracted few headlines, even though persistent problems of dealing with health finance contractors have bedeviled the program's managers for years. The straitjackets in which managers often find themselves as a result of congressional strictures often make it hard for them to solve either kind of problem, and Congress tends not to look carefully at what kind of problem it might have on its hands.

In short, congressional behavior is the source of many of our performance problems, and to reverse this syndrome, Congress must develop a stronger institutional capacity to examine management problems. It also needs to create stronger incentives for agency managers to focus on long-term performance. Members of Congress will naturally continue to focus on passing horror stories where they find them, but they would significantly improve management if they put these stories into broader perspective.

Members of Congress must recognize more clearly the links between their actions and the management problems of federal programs. Short-term attention to intermittent scandals, coupled with a profound unwillingness to allow federal agencies to build the management capacity they need, can only encourage reactive management and new problems. No matter how hard executive branch managers work to improve long-term government performance, they need sustained leadership from members of Congress if they are to succeed.

Therefore, the congressional committee originating each new or significantly changed program should produce a management impact statement to be included in the committee's report on the legislation.

The management impact statement would identify the important management issues that program changes would raise. Such a statement would ensure that Congress consid-

ers carefully the administrative as well as the policy implications of each new program. It would also ensure that
Congress clearly focuses the executive branch's attention
on the management issues it views as most important in any
new program.

Controlling Discretion through Internal Procedures

No matter how effectively OMB and Congress balance
the external control of bureaucracy with the need for operating flexibility, problems of bureaucratic power will inevitably remain. This has led to a focus on how to structure
internal controls of bureaucracy.

Market-based theories, devoted to understanding and
designing institutional structures, have produced new ways
of thinking about the inner workings of bureaucracy. Embracing the work of microeconomic theorists and rational-
choice political scientists, these analysts are variously known
as New Theorists, Coasean economists (after Nobel laure-
ate Ronald Coase), or transaction-cost theorists.[6] The gist
of their thinking is that organizations and those who work
in them seek to minimize their costs and maximize gains.
Thus they develop tactics to promote greater worker accountability and improve organizational performance. Some
theorists have adapted the New Theory to the public sector.
The traditional mechanistic models of Frederick Winslow
Taylor and Max Weber seek the most efficient transmission
of orders from the top to the bottom of a bureaucracy. The
New Theorists, however, envision bureaucracy as a series
of special contractual relationships between superiors and
subordinates. Bureaucracy for them is fundamentally a
market-based, not authority-based, system. The task of the
manager is to improve organizational performance by solving the recurring problems of this primary transaction.
Three concepts—transaction costs, the employment contract, and information—are crucial to this analysis.

In hiring and supervising employees, supervisors begin
by making a fundamental transaction: pay in exchange for

services. Like all smart managers, they seek the best returns for the costs they must incur.[7] Getting good information on every transaction (say, on every action taken by subordinates) is very difficult, of course. Managers therefore try to reduce their costs by lumping together a series of these transactions into a single macrocontract. The classic example is the contract that employees negotiate with an employer. It is impossible reasonably to cover all contingencies because the transaction costs would be exorbitant. Instead, workers and managers establish a hierarchy. Employees agree within reason to follow the instructions of the superior. Superiors who wish to minimize transaction costs give employees automatic raises so long as they do as they are told when on the job. To the New Theorists, the civil service general schedule is itself just a special, albeit a particularly rigid and encompassing, type of employment contract.

Within this contract, employees are hired as agents of the owners of the firm. Civil servants can be considered agents of elected officials and of their organizational superiors. As the federal bureaucracy has expanded, more and more layers of principals and agents have been added, producing the pyramidal structure that is conventionally cited to describe the government's hierarchy. However, as the number of layers has grown, organizational distance between nonadjacent layers has increased and information losses have become more common and more difficult to solve.

From this information problem the New Theorists have developed fresh concerns about bureaucratic power. When superiors cannot be sure what their subordinates are doing, and when subordinates' goals differ from those of their superiors, subordinates will follow their interests rather than those of the organization. For this reason, New Theorists identify a problem of renegade bureaucratic discretion that seems not to have greatly troubled the Progressives. Woodrow Wilson believed that the representativeness and expertise of government management would create a civil service "so intimately connected with the popular thought, by means of elections and constant public counsel, as to find arbitrariness or class spirit quite out of the question."[8] The New Theorists argue that class spirit is unavoidable.

Professionalism once implied a heightened level of attention to the value of academic credentials, a stiffening of intellectual and professional standards, an emphasis on the ethos of a discipline as well as on its technical lore. It would have been contrary to civil servants' professional training and ethics to substitute their own policies for those specified by political superiors. Thus did the belief in professionalism and the so-called policy-administration dichotomy make their way into the early canon of public administration theory. Then early in the twentieth century Frank Gilbreth, a leader in Taylor's scientific management movement, popularized the doctrine that "one best way" could be discovered to do any job. Conscientious administrators' knowledge of the best way would leave them with no choice but to apply standard accounting procedures or whatever other way of tackling problems represented the state of the art in their fields of expertise.[9]

But the New Theorists emphasize that expertise also has a downside, the term for which is *asymmetric information*. Asymmetric information occurs when the agents in an organization know more than their principals do about the business at hand. It is a particularly acute problem in organizations characterized by large organizational distances, and hence serial information losses, and in which staff members must possess expertise to process large volumes of technical data. Those who possess expertise can develop shortcuts through approved procedures. Bureaucrats can also use their specialized information to erect defenses against intrusion by outsiders and even against close scrutiny within the organization. In these circumstances, it also becomes relatively easy for them to abuse the discretionary power that they all possess in some degree. Conditions of asymmetric information thus become the preconditions for the appearance of what New Theorists call the agency problem.

According to the New Theorists, then, almost any large, technically oriented organization may be filled with recesses into which bureaucrats can retreat to bend rules unobserved. The same may be said of far-flung direct-service organizations in which street-level bureaucrats—police, case workers, parole officers, and the like—are expected to implement policy but must do so largely without direct supervision. This phenomenon encourages managers to seek control over their subordinates by writing ever more elaborate rules. Not surprisingly, what results is a thicket of agency-specific housekeeping regulations, local customs, behavioral codes, established practices, and standard operating procedures that make it seem bureaucracy is in business for itself, not the public.

As a result, bureaucracy tends to become ever more self-contained, inner directed, and balkanized. We have built a system that maximizes control but delivers little accountability.[10] When federal managers are asked to identify the impediments to improving their performance, they point to rules and restrictions imposed by other organizational units (or by Congress). "We could do far better, and save much money," they claim, "if the secretary gave us more flexibility in procurement [or personnel, or spending] policy." If the monitors of those rules are questioned, they reply that they "know more about important details than the operating agencies. If operating divisions have more discretion they will only produce more problems." Most federal rules, they point out, are designed to ensure that past problems are not repeated. Everyone agrees that we need to reform government, but that the problems and thus the responsibility for doing so lie elsewhere.

In the face of attacks over poor performance, blaming others is understandable. But reactive management will never solve the problem. Instead,

government managers from top to bottom must take personal responsibility for government performance.

The lesson taught by the New Theory is that government bureaucrats will not tackle performance problems until those problems become *their* problems to solve, until their "class spirit" includes programmatic issues as well as personal concerns. Making that happen is the foremost job of top government managers.

Worker Quality and Motivation

Analysts of bureaucracy often contend that the deck seems stacked against administrators, that the personnel system has few incentives to encourage quality work. Although the civil service classification of positions has always been controversial, doubts about its value and workability have grown rapidly in recent years. Under the terms of the general schedule, the government must at least pay employees at the specified pay levels, almost irrespective of their diligence. It is a situation inviting what the New Theorists call adverse selection, a situation that attracts candidates who seek career cushions rather than career challenges. A civil service applicant might be motivated by the desire to serve. But the motivation might also lie in the attractiveness of a job with regular salary increases and virtual immunity from firing unless underperformance becomes flagrant. Once applicants have been taken into the classified service, New Theorists argue, job security regardless of performance cannot help but tempt civil servants to shirk. Such behavior illustrates the "moral hazard" phenomenon, a term coined in the insurance industry for people's tendency to exercise less care if an insurer will indemnify negligent behavior.

Although these theories have been criticized by many academics, they help us understand that certain patterns of behavior in public bureaucracies are functions of bureaucratic structures and procedures. The New Theorists' hypotheses rest on simple assumptions: people seek to behave rationally, and it is rational to work less if it can be done for the same pay. The theories of adverse selection and moral hazard play directly to many Americans' stereotypes of civil servants as faceless bureaucrats—overpaid, underworked, marching in lockstep, and enjoying tenure guarantees that remove any incentive for excellence. No wonder the confident bureaucracy building of the Progressives became the bureaucracy bashing of the 1980s.

Efforts to improve government performance ultimately have to deal with these problems of bureaucratic culture.

Top officials, in particular, must promote within their agencies a culture that values a proactive, problem-solving attitude to replace the reactive, problem-avoiding attitude that too often dominates the federal bureaucracy.

There will always be critical information gaps, and the behavior of employees can never be completely supervised. But a problem-solving attitude imparted to workers throughout the bureaucracy can promote performance, reduce transaction costs, and reduce the information burdens of government managers.

Three Special Concerns

Our analysis of the historical roots and current complexities of bureaucratic problems identifies three special concerns:

—*Federal responsibilities versus capabilities*. The responsibilities of bureaucracy have outstripped public managers' capacity for effective management.

—*Organizational distance and complexity*. The bureaucracy has both vertical and horizontal problems. Vertically, it is a multilayered hierarchy riddled with surveillance-proof recesses and vulnerable to information losses. Horizontally, it is a patchwork of functionally specialized agencies in which efforts to coordinate activities with other agencies can consume as much energy as an agency's primary functions.

—*Federal workers and their workplace*. The federal

workplace is overgrown with rules. It is buffered against deregulation by layers of interlocking statutes, judicial interpretations, rulemakings under the Administrative Procedures Act, and customary interpretations of agency regulations. And it is characterized by a bureaucratic culture of lassitude and risk-aversiveness.

Solving these problems requires solving three social puzzles. First, we must determine which problems are public problems and which should remain in the private sector. Second, among public problems, we must determine which are federal problems and which should be left to state and local governments and then how to coordinate the different pieces of the federal bureaucracy that play a role in solving them. Finally, in managing the federal role, we must create a workpace that can efficiently get the job done.

A high-performance federal bureaucracy requires structural changes at all three levels in this system of Chinese boxes. In chapters 4 and 5 we look at the first question by examining the division of labor between the public and private sectors. In chapter 6 we probe the organizational boundaries of the federal bureaucracy to answer the second question. In chapter 7 we assess personnel and workplace rules to answer the third question. We conclude the book in chapter 8 by examining how these perspectives can be combined to create a fresh entrepreneurial culture. Therein lies the key to reinvigorating the federal government and improving government performance.

4

The Federal Government's Responsibilities

THE GRADUAL ASSUMPTION by the federal government of private sector functions, as described in chapter 2, may well have been consistent with the Progressives' original design. But government's capacity to manage its burdens has failed to keep pace with the lengthening list of public responsibilities. Improving government performance thus demands a careful assessment of the responsibilities that government should be asked to undertake in the first place, and then of the management capacities required to discharge its responsibilities in an effective and democratically accountable manner.

We may even further shrink the responsibilities assigned to government agencies, although the trend since World War II has been to expand governmental responsibility and to rely increasingly on public-private partnerships to provide services. What we are not likely to change is a subtle but important change in the federal government's basic role. Before World War II the federal government delivered many of its services itself through federal agencies and federal workers. As the federal government's responsibilities have broadened, its partnerships with state and local governments, nonprofit organizations, and private contractors have multiplied. The federal government's role consequently has dramatically changed. It is now far less involved in direct retail of its programs; is far more involved in wholesaling its services by acting as financier, arranger, and overseer, but not direct provider. This changed role has altered and in some ways increased its management responsibilities. At any conceivable level of government operations, and regardless of the degree of devolution that might occur, the federal government will need improved management capabilities.

Dividing the Job

The Progressives believed not only in bureaucracy (that is, in rationally designed structures staffed by experts) but in public bureaucracy. Certain functions, they believed, simply had to be performed in public agencies, not by private firms. Indeed, allowing those functions to remain in private hands would sacrifice the public interest to narrow private interests. Even today, certain services can (and probably must) be provided directly by government. These mainly include

—services commonly deemed to be inherently governmental (making foreign policy and deploying military forces abroad);

—services that call for special levels of public accountability (police work, parole and probation);

—services that can be routinized for mass delivery (disbursing social security and food stamp benefits).

Today's advocates of privatization and contracting out argue that public agencies as we know them may no longer be up to some of the jobs for which they were originally created, let alone for many of the additional tasks that have been assigned to government as the residual solver of the nation's economic and social problems. The argument for adjusting the balance of publicly and privately delivered services supposes an outlook unencumbered by assumptions about the special worthiness of public sector activity. It calls for a broad view of the demand for goods and services across the entire economy and then decisions about the institutions that have comparative advantages in providing different products.

For the past few decades, but especially during the Reagan years, the capacity of the federal government to manage well has come under systematic attack. If government is too big, too inefficient, and too overloaded with inappropriate functions, the obvious answer is to transfer responsibility to the private sector where competitive markets can promote efficiency, either through more contracting out or through outright privatization. The New Theorists support this approach by arguing that rule-bound bureaucracies increase transaction costs and hence make service delivery less efficient.

Reforming the Federal Procurement System

Contracting out and privatization represent different ways of allocating three functions between the public sector and the private: decisionmaking (someone must choose whether to provide a given service and at what level), financing (someone must arrange to provide the resources needed to satisfy the production function for the product in question), and implementation (someone must oversee actual production and manage the delivery of services to customers). Privatization moves all three functions into the private sector. With contracting out, the production decision and the financing process remain within the public sector, at least in theory, but much of implementation is delegated to private agents.

That, at least, is the theory. In practice, however, federal contracting is plagued by at least three problems. Some contractors make decisions that ought to be left to government officials. Contractors make these decisions because the federal government does not have the capacity to make the decisions itself. Finally, the contracting process is complicated by a maze of regulations.

In many programs private contractors make important decisions as well as implement them. Contractors for the

Department of Energy, for example, have prepared testimony for agency officials to present before congressional committees. EPA contractors have also answered the agency's Superfund hotline and advised callers about which projects might be eligible for funding. Other contractors have helped develop the Department of Transportation's safety policy. Each involvement meant using the discretion granted federal bureaus by Congress and shaping fundamental policy decisions, decisions that easily could be viewed as inherently governmental. At EPA, in fact, contractors developed criteria for how the agency ought to define inherently governmental functions that should not be contracted out.[11]

Relying on contractors to deliver services is one thing; relying on them to make government policy is another. Many federal agencies lack the staff, in numbers or training, to conduct such work. Sometimes, as with the Superfund program, these shortages flow directly from congressional restrictions on agency hiring. Drawing the line between policy execution and policymaking, moreover, is difficult. Public administration has been struggling for a century, with increasing frustration, to solve this problem. Nevertheless, as the government's central manager, the Office of Management and Budget must ensure that government officials exercise public discretion.

The director of OMB should strengthen the guidance provided to federal agencies about which functions can be assigned to contractors and which ones must never be contracted out.

The contracting issue, however, extends far past the basic question of what the government should contract out and what it should not. The federal government has always relied on private contractors for producing government services. In the past generation, however, the government's reliance on private contractors, through so-called service contracts, for the information on which public decisions are based has increased dramatically. The government's investment in monitoring and evaluating the results of its programs has dropped just as dramatically. What it knows it frequently must glean from self-reporting by its own contractors or from contractors hired to oversee other contractors. The information for making basic public decisions is increasingly flowing to private contractors.[12] For example, the Defense Nuclear Facilities Safety Board, which advises the secretary of energy on the management of the nation's defense nuclear complex, has worried that "the most important and far-reaching problem affecting the safety of DOE defense nuclear facilities is the difficulty in attracting and retaining personnel who are adequately qualified by technical education and experience to provide the kind of management, direction, and guidance essential to safe operation of DOE's defense nuclear facilities."[13] DOE itself is but an administrative shell; its contractors do the actual work, and as much as 90 percent of its budget is spent through them. Because of the expertise of the contractors, DOE's problems in maintaining its own expertise, and the long tradition of contractor autonomy, effective supervision of contractors has been difficult. As a result, conflicts of interest, poor performance, and cost overruns have been legion.

While DOE's problems are among the very worst in the federal government, the basic pattern has been replicated throughout.[14] If the federal government is to rely on private contractors to deliver many of its services (and that is a given in the complexity of today's world), it must rebuild its capacity to make the basic decisions of governance: to set basic policy and to oversee the results that contractors produce. If it does not, the government's ability to govern will erode. Private contractors will make important public decisions.

Congress and the president should together devote greater resources to strengthening the fundamental capacity of government agencies to oversee their contractors.

Finally, the contracting process is plagued by a confusing welter of rules. These rules are intended to ensure fairness to all competitors and strict accountability for those who win government contracts. They are, however, so complex that they produce perverse consequences. Federal acquisition regulations and the armed services procurement regulations fill tens of thousands of pages. They allow procurement officers little discretion to use initiative. The military specification for fruitcake, adopted in 1980, for example, ran to eighteen pages. It defined, among other things, the size of nuts and the procedures for soaking the raisins.

In private contracting, organizations look for reliable suppliers of quality goods at reasonable prices. In public contracting, regulations to avoid political favoritism insist on a compartmentalized bidding process that most private companies would find ludicrous. It is even rare that successful past performance by a contractor can be considered, let alone rewarded, when competitive bids for new government work are assessed. The result is a system that too often delivers goods too late, at too high a price, and too inadequate to do the job. Unsurprisingly, public sector buyers are far more frequently dissatisfied than their private sector counterparts with the performance of their vendors. "Public officials cannot use common sense and good judgement in ways that would promote better vendor performance," Steven Kelman has noted. The system "should be significantly deregulated to allow public officials greater discretion."[15]

As the number and complexity of the rules written to control the federal contracting process have increased, so have the responsibilities of the auditors and investigators who are supposed to ensure compliance with the rules. It would be difficult to overstate the pervasiveness of the control-oriented auditing and investigative sensitivity among seasoned civil servants. The cautious attitude among procurement specialists suggests that the threats of auditing and investigation do in fact deter much of the corruption and carelessness that might otherwise occur in the federal contracting process. The problem is, however, that this caution interferes with the necessary work of government.

No mechanical fix is possible. No universal formulation can be advanced to guide procurement policies throughout the federal establishment. The necessity for incremental evolutionary change is especially pertinent here. The government needs to experiment with granting procurement managers more flexibility in negotiating with vendors and greater ability to take past performance instead of only current bids into account when awarding contracts. Several high-visibility, carefully monitored demonstration programs should be used immediately as tests of an improved contracting-out regime and used eventually as models for reforming the mechanics of the procurement process. Procurement officials should be allowed to have far more influence than is now the case. This experiment should allow procurement managers increased discretion, balanced by written justification of the decision and scrutiny by multimember review panels.

Congress should mandate a series of experiments, monitored by OMB's director of federal procurement, that authorize federal procurement officials to award contracts based on past experience with contractors.

Remaking the General Services Administration

No effort to reform federal procurement can succeed without parallel efforts to improve the operations of the federal government's own central purchasing agent and landlord, the General Services Administration (GSA). The idea promoted by the first Hoover commission, that consolidated management of purchasing and building space could produce substantial economies of scale, has not been fully realized. The tug of war continues; GSA presses for centralized control of purchasing, and officials who depend on the agency for supplies and building maintenance complain of its inefficiency and red tape. While federal agencies struggle to make do with less, they find that the rents GSA charges steadily go up.

Agency managers frequently want to select their own buildings, purchase their own pencils, and allocate their own parking spaces. More important, they want greater authority to manage their own computing and telecommunications services. The federal government's needs have become too varied and the options in the electronic marketplace too complex and changing to allow for traditional central purchasing. The budget and work force cuts made by Congress and OMB during the 1980s did lead to decentralization of some activities. And congressional restrictions on procurement tie GSA's hands. Agencies are required to purchase from the federal supply schedule even though delivery times are longer and prices often higher than if they were allowed to buy supplies in the private market. Nevertheless, GSA has remained plagued by recurring scandals, too understaffed to be genuinely important in procurement, yet locked in that role by its own culture and by congressional demands.

GSA can continue to be important in providing basic information about the government's purchasing needs, from office supplies to electronic equipment. However,

Congress should authorize federal agencies to assume most of the purchasing responsibilities previously held by GSA. To fit its new role, GSA needs to transform itself from a centralized, control-oriented agency to a service agency and strategic planner more attuned to the needs of its own customers, the federal agencies.

That will require substantial leadership by GSA's top managers as they seek to match the agency's mission to the technical realities of the government's needs and today's marketplace.

Revitalizing Federalism

Through a steady march of programs, the federal government has come to rely increasingly on state and local governments as its partners in domestic policy. Presidential initiatives have more self-consciously made the federal government the wholesaler of services for which state and local governments, often in concert with nonprofit organizations and private contractors, have become the retailers. The pattern is illustrated in some of the most far-reaching statutory arrangements in our system: the shared social security financing and payment arrangements under the Social Security Act (administered by the states subject to federal review for compliance with minimum standards set by the secretary of health and human services); the mandates for active state and local participation in land use planning under the Federal Land Policy and Management Act (regionally administered subject to federal review for compliance with minimum planning criteria set by the secretary of the Department of Interior); and the state implementation plan provisions of the Clean Air Act, under which state officials develop specific plans for environmental cleanup (subject to minimum standards set by the EPA administrator). From welfare to economic development, health care to transportation, toxic waste cleanup to environmental policy, the federal, state, and local governments have developed ever closer ties. The pattern, a familiar one for decades, has become even more important in the 1990s.

Today, because the federal government acts as a dispenser of conditional legal authorities to others and then as the check writer, financial intermediary, service packager, and program overseer on which the entire system depends, the structure of government services differs from what it was even a few decades ago. Despite the changes since World War II, however, the federal government remains organized for the jobs of the 1950s. It also remains organized as if its job were to serve the rural-urban mix of citizens involved in the same industrial patterns that prevailed forty years ago. Much of what passes for inefficiency in intergovernmental programs is the result of structures and practices that time has simply distanced from the functions that federal bureaucrats must actually perform.

This quiet revolution in American federalism is a healthy and encouraging one. The state and local governments have become more than equal to the job, a stark transformation from the days when they were the backwater of the intergovernmental system. Some of the most lively and hopeful policy innovations in the United States, including bold experiments in welfare and health care reform, have welled up from the states. Nevertheless, the federal government often continues to treat its state and local partners as children who must be constantly supervised. Today's world calls for structural, programmatic, and philosophical adjustments in federal-state-local relationships.

Whenever consistent with administration and the law, cabinet secretaries should grant waivers to allow state and local governments to experiment with innovative programs.

Federalism also needs a high-level voice within the executive branch.

The president should emphasize the importance of federalism by including the director of the U.S. Advisory Commission on Intergovernmental Relations on the Domestic Policy Council.

5

Rebuilding Government Capacity

DESPITE THE LARGER ROLES that the federal government's contractors and intergovernmental partners have assumed, the list of functions it is responsible for is likely to become longer, not shorter. In fact, as new problems arise there is a greater tendency to look to government to solve them and for government to rely on complex partnerships to do the job. Notwithstanding the growing role of nonfederal partners in federal programs, citizens seem unlikely to forgive presidents, members of Congress, or anyone else who happens to live and work in Washington if the programs are poorly planned, carelessly implemented, or (worst of all) ignored altogether. Even if a private-nonprofit, or governmental partner ends up with the ultimate assignment to provide a given service at retail, it will remain some federal official'a obligation to ensure that the job is done right. For this reason, privatization, contracting out, and devolved federalism all promise to increase the need for sound planning and effective oversight of federal programs.

But the record shows scant recognition of this requirement. Consider only recent history: Jimmy Carter, Ronald Reagan, George Bush, and Bill Clinton all ran against Washington. In the past two decades this struggle against the capital establishment has become a war of attrition, eroding the morale of the public servants who manage government programs. To many the mandate to cut the size of government and contract out functions did no more than recognize the imperatives of the age, but the gradual erosion of public capacity has left us with a government overly dependent on private contractors. That trend raises profound worries about whose interests will be put foremost.

Reductions in the federal government's capacity to monitor, assess, and correct errors in programs entrusted to nonfederal providers helped produce fraud in medicare, the flawed Hubble space telescope, some of the worst defense procurement scandals ever, skyrocketing defaults in the guaranteed student loan program, excessive costs in the Superfund, and malfeasance of Teapot Dome proportions in the Department of Housing and Urban Development. Problems have grown, the House of Representatives Committee on Government Operations concluded, "due in large part to a lack of commitment to sound and efficient management."[16]

Smarter, Not Bigger, Government

We may not need a bigger federal government, and the trends toward increased federal wholesaling and load shedding may be promising signs of our adaptability. But we do need a smarter government, one better equipped to shape coherent policies, to follow through with coordinated implementation, to evaluate interim results and ensure a continuing process of constructive evolution.

What does it mean to say we need a smarter government? It means that the federal government must improve its informational and analytical capabilities by establishing a solid financial management information system, installing hardware and software systems that will put federal workers on a solid technological footing, recasting the federal budget in terms that better link spending with performance, and rethinking the role of the staff agencies that provide the core budgeting and personnel services. Specifically, we must develop a better central nervous system within OMB; we must transform the role of the Office of Personnel Management (OPM) to chart the government's future personnel needs; we must invest in leadership and executive management training programs, especially for federal middle managers (GS-12 to GS-15); and we must redesign the responsibilities of the officials who oversee the government's functions and better train them to do their jobs.

Strengthening Financial Management

In the Department of Agriculture's food stamp program, about $100 million of benefits is illegally diverted annually. The Department of Energy is spending billions to clean up environmental problems at its nuclear weapons plants, but the cleanup has been plagued by cost overruns and poor performance. Inadequate controls compromise the expenditure of billions of dollars in the Environmental Protection Agency's Superfund program. A hundred similar high-risk problems abound, according to OMB's own studies. OMB, in fact, has had to dispatch "SWAT teams" to the field to help solve the most serious problems.[17] Indeed, no federal department or agency seems to be exempt from the problems, and the potential costs are huge.

These problems are rooted in financial management weaknesses that impair the ability of managers to manage, of leaders to lead. Needed is a system that provides timely information about what money is being spent for which projects and, most important, with what results. To this end in 1990 Congress passed the Chief Financial Officers Act, which mandated the appointment of chief financial officers in all major federal agencies and established a new deputy director for management and a controller within OMB to oversee government finances. The act also required the preparation of financial statements for a handful of pilot agencies, the performance of audits by inspectors general, and the drafting of a long-term improvement plan. Despite the act's great promise, results have fallen short. OMB has just thirty-two people on its staff to deal with financial management for the $1.5 trillion the federal government spends annually. In some agencies, the financial management job was added to the portfolio of already overburdened, and sometimes inadequately experienced, assistant secretaries for management. Improved financial management is no panacea, but it is a critical building block for better performance.

The director of OMB should vigorously implement the Chief Financial Officers Act of 1990 by closely monitoring agencies' compliance with the act and by seeking additional financial support from Congress, if necessary.

Upgrading Technology

The government has for years underinvested in computers, as President Clinton discovered when he moved into the White House. For example, the Resolution Trust Corporation, charged with selling $400 billion in assets from failed thrift institutions, was crippled by its inability to track acquisitions and dispositions of assets. The $13 billion student loan program is plagued by missing and incomplete data. Applicants for programs managed by the Department of Agriculture complain about having to fill out duplicate forms for closely related programs. USDA employees reply that they have no choice because the department's computer system does not allow them to exchange information easily. Fraud has been endemic in the medicare program, in part because of an inadequate computer system. Nothing in this record bodes well for the national health care system.

Succeeding waves of top-level appointees are frustrated by what they find when they arrive, yet they spend little time thinking strategically about how to prevent the problems from recurring. Mismanagement of technology in particular is in part a reflection of a broader inattention within government to management in general. Top political appointees rarely stay long in their positions, so they focus their attention on issues of high policy where they can quickly make their mark. Under the pressures of short time and overwhelming demands, they can easily overlook the importance of information technology for their agencies. The right kind of technology, when used with effective management information systems, can shorten organizational distance and reduce the information problems from which many management mistakes originate.

Some of the problem is the result of poor decisions by procurement officers. Twice in the past twenty-five years the Internal Revenue Service has attempted to modernize its computer capacities; twice the results were sluggish systems not up to the job. Other problems have dogged the Social Security Administration and the Federal Aviation Administration, both of which depend heavily on computers. Some of the problem comes from the budget and procurement process. As the General Accounting Office pointed out, procurement

> demands certainty and is risk-averse, yet [computer] systems development is inherently uncertain and risk-intensive. The process calls for systems developers to formulate precise long-term plans and budgets. It unrealistically assumes that detailed systems requirements can be well understood at the outset, that software development will be predictable, and that long-term budgeting can be done with a high degree of accuracy. Unfortunately, none of these expectations recognizes the enormous difficulties involved in developing large systems.[18]

Responsibility for overseeing the government's management rests with OMB and especially with its deputy director for management. The deputy director needs to strengthen the agency's management information office and to ensure that the government plans strategically to meet the demands it faces. In particular,

the deputy director of OMB, in concert with the president's science adviser and in consultation with the Office of Technology Assessment, should develop a master blueprint for the federal government's information management needs and technology.

Performance Budgeting

The federal government lacks adequate capacity to define goals, measure results, and relate them to spending in any but the most impressionistic, nonrigorous ways.[19] This deficiency is profound, for it makes it impossible to define what performance truly means or to measure how well the government is doing. Two-thirds of the agencies surveyed by GAO in 1992 said they had strategic plans, and three-fourths claimed to collect performance data. The information they had, however, was far from what would be needed to construct a true performance budget. Almost no agencies sought explicitly to connect their strategic plans with long-term objectives or to link their objectives to measurable outputs.[20]

Thus far the most significant proposal for linking the budget with performance has been Senator William V. Roth's Government Performance and Results Act (Senate bill 20). Senator Roth has campaigned for years to establish a performance-based budget system for the federal government. His bill would mandate performance measurement throughout the federal bureaucracy. Each agency would be required to frame a five-year strategic plan defining its mission and long-term goals, breaking long-term goals into short-term objectives, identifying benchmarks by which progress toward the short-term objectives could be judged, and issuing an annual report on its progress. Although the

Roth proposal speaks to the need for major reform, it takes a relatively modest first step. It recognizes that even sweeping change is often best accomplished by steps—experimentally, incrementally. Ten pilot projects would be completed and evaluated by OMB in 2001 before the act took effect governmentwide.

Although the pace is moderate, it is worth remembering that proposals for a federal performance budget date from the 1913 Taft commission report. In the meantime other budget reforms (notably planning-programming-budgeting, management by objectives, and zero-base budgeting) have risen and fallen. The federal government's experience with these reforms teaches several important lessons. First, the technical burden of following sensible recommendations is daunting: defining goals and translating them into measurable performance benchmarks are deceptively tough tasks. Second, getting objectives to sit still so long-term plans can be made is difficult in the world of Washington politics. Third, getting anyone to care about the planning process is hard. It rarely produces quick results. Indeed, the strategic focus is explicitly designed to avoid sacrificing long-term results for fleeting progress. Under the press of day-to-day policy struggles, sustained attention to program budgeting is hard for either the president or members of Congress to muster. Fourth, federal employees must be included as full partners in the effort. Too often reforms have been seen as end runs around the bureaucracy. They tend to fail unless government employees have an important say. Fifth, how new procedures are introduced is often more important than what they are designed to accomplish. Building confidence in the process is usually the first requirement for achieving results.

Performance budgeting is not likely to prove a silver bullet, but the case for movement in the direction of the Roth reform is compelling. Therefore,

the president should embrace and the Congress should pass Senate bill 20 now.

Serving Customers and Total Quality Management

The objection so many citizens have to bureaucrats derives, quite simply, from the conviction that they seem primarily concerned with meeting their own needs, not those of citizens. Government too often seems in business for itself, or perhaps for some special interest with special access to decisions. The total quality management (TQM) movement has sought to transform government by making it more customer oriented.

Although the idea of focusing on citizens as customers has attracted many fans, it has rankled some experts on administration. H. George Frederickson, for example, has protested that citizens are the owners, not the customers, of government. In Frederickson's view the job of public administrators is to ensure that the government's power is used to execute the law, not to transfer power to either bureaucrats or citizens in a way that could undermine the democratic process.[21] Would making government more responsive to customers mean that the loudest get served the first and best, that poorly represented citizens could have their voices ignored? This is a serious issue in light of widespread concern by scholars and ordinary citizens over interest penetration and special-interest politics. Would decentralizing decisions in order to serve citizens as customers require sacrificing uniformity in policymaking? Organizational complexity, after all, already makes incoherence in policymaking one of the critical challenges of federal performance.

Despite these complexities, there is one overriding reality. Citizens expect to be treated as customers, with responsiveness and consideration. That is as much true at the social security office as it is at the supermarket. Despite its indisputable attraction, however, the idea that government should focus more on its customers is far more complex than it at first appears. Four and competing approaches drive government in four different directions in seeking to serve the customer (figure 2).

REBUILDING GOVERNMENT CAPACITY   49

Figure 2. The Customers of Government

"Customer"	Perspective
Citizens as service recipients	Responsiveness
Partners in service provision	Effectiveness
Overseers of performance	Accountability
Citizens as taxpayers	Efficiency

The Citizen as Service Recipient

Government is in business, of course, to serve its citizens, to provide goods and services that elected officials have decided are in the public interest. Citizens want those goods and services to be responsive; they want their needs to take priority over the needs of those who are providing the goods and services. This is a close corollary of the private sector's TQM approach, which holds that customers ultimately determine quality. In government, an approach to quality and performance builds on one fundamental precept: to make citizens the focus of service and to make responsiveness to them a primary goal.

Partners in Service Provision

As state and local governments, native American tribal governments, nonprofit organizations, and private sector organizations have come to be more prominent partners in delivering federal programs, a customer-centered approach to government must take their needs into account as well. The same is true of the needs of federal managers who must make the partnerships work. Fitting all these pieces together neatly is critical to making programs effective. Indeed, as the federal government's wholesale role has grown, the importance of working closely with its partners has increased. These partners are intermediate customers; the federal government needs to serve them well if citizens are to be served. Truly effective services require making the service delivery system seamless. Citizens care far less about the name of the agency on the door than that their problems are solved. For example, a 1992 study assessed how best to improve the quality of services programs managed by the Department of Health and Human Services: to develop new service delivery structures and programs or to link clients with existing services through collocating service providers and using case managers. The result? Case management and collocation proved far more effective.[22] To pursue that approach, however, requires that the process itself and the federal government's partners in that process become customers.

Overseers of Performance

Responding to citizens as service recipients is not the only goal of government. Federal agencies live under the basic tenet of American democracy: government bureaucracies and the programs they manage are creatures of the legislature, under the supervision of the executive, and subject to review by the courts. These overseers expect and are due accountability, both financial and programmatic. Frequently, of course, the perspectives of these overseers overlap with the interests of citizens as customers. That, however, is not guaranteed, especially if some customers dominate a program to the exclusion of others. The reality is that this accountability takes political, legal, and ethical precedence over paying attention to citizens as service recipients.

Citizens as Taxpayers

Ultimately, all citizens are indeed owners of the process because they pay the bills. Quite apart from their role as service recipients, they expect high-quality government services at low costs. There is a paradox here, of course. The emphasis on efficiency typically applies to those programs citizens do not themselves receive. When they are the focus of a program, no expenditure can seem enough, as reformers in health and education policy have discovered. Still, there is indisputable truth in the citizens-as-owners argument. Citizens pay taxes just as surely as they receive benefits. As taxpayers they expect and deserve efficiency in government.

Responsiveness, effectiveness, accountability, and efficiency cannot all be balanced evenly, simultaneously, or permanently. The effort to improve government performance is important, but understanding it requires working through a series of complications. First, any government program or agency has multiple customers with multiple levels of interest. These customers and interests, moreover, frequently change. Charting the process helps identify who is likely to appear as a customer.

Second, different customers are likely to have very different ideas about how they ought to be served, and these ideas are likely to be different in turn from those of service providers. Some of the serve-the-customer rhetoric seems to assume that the task is relatively uniform. In fact, given the multiple customers of government programs, conflict among them about what programs ought to accomplish is likely to be constant. Unlike the private sector, moreover, government agencies usually cannot choose their customers. Establishing situations in which everyone wins will not always be possible. What is most important is to create an ongoing relationship of trust, not necessarily to satisfy every customer. Managing conflict and speaking clearly about what can be done, what cannot be done, and why has to be the core of the government's job.

A third complication is that some customers will have a hard time finding their way to the service. Political power in the United States is scarcely uniform, and some have far greater resources than others. One of government's jobs is to recognize those who might be disenfranchised by power politics and to represent them at the table. That might mean providing the resources to bring them to the table or to recognize surrogates to speak for them. If a customer-centered process is to be seen as legitimate, it must be fair.

Fourth, there are many intermediate customers. Because of the complexity of government programs and the multiple steps required to go from program design to execution, many customers have other customers. That means they rely heavily on the integrity of the process, from top to bottom. How well citizens are treated depends on how well the process works along the way.

As a fifth complication, the job of serving the customer means not only making individual programs more responsive but also integrating programs so that the junctures appear seamless. Citizens do not care that many federal agencies provide loan programs for rural development. What they do care about is that when they need a loan they can get it with a minimum of inconvenience. Government is built from programs and agencies. Each program and agency, quite naturally, has its own boundaries. Without such boundaries, there would be no limit to the managers' responsibilities and no way to hold them accountable. At the same time, however, these boundaries can build impediments to effective governance. They can encourage government officials to ignore the natural connections among government programs and agencies, to look defensively inward to deny responsibility instead of aggressively outward to solve problems. These boundaries, in turn, can create barriers to citizens seeking to match their needs with what government offers. As a result, government too often appears to be in business for itself instead of being in business to serve citizens. Adding all these complications together emphasizes that

all government workers, regardless of their level, must strive vigorously and ceaselessly to make customer service, not their own needs, the focus of their activity.

In focusing more on its customers the federal government has also begun moving more toward total quality management. TQM relies on an organization's employees as the source of ideas for improvement. The movement's proponents contend that government officials on the front lines know best what their customers' problems are and how to solve them. It follows that granting officials more discretion to solve problems on their own and in creative new ways is the key to improved government performance. It is an appealing clutch of ideas. Indeed, the very label, promising to devote management to the total pursuit of quality results, has helped sell the ideas.

The TQM effort within the federal government, however, is a mile wide and an inch deep. In one survey, managers in 68 percent of all federal installations were working on TQM. Just 13 percent of their employees, though, were actively involved with efforts to promote the reform. Agencies moving toward TQM reported that performance in fact improved, and that improvement accelerated as TQM matured. At the same time, there were significant barriers. Many employees did not believe that they had the power to make changes. Training in TQM information and methods was often thin.[23]

Cautious managers, fearful of having government enthusiastically embrace yet another private sector innovation just as the private sector begins moving away from it, have trod uneasily. TQM has worked best in businesses that have clearly identifiable products and where quality is relatively easy to judge. In manufacturing, some of the early enthusiasm for TQM has ebbed. Embracing quality as the most important goal within a given business does not always guarantee higher profits, and implementing TQM can involve a greater investment than some managers finally think worthwhile. In service organizations, including most public agencies, goals are harder to define and outputs fuzzier than they are in manufacturing where the movement enjoyed its principal successes.

Nevertheless, as analyst James E. Swiss has pointed out, adapting TQM to government offers genuine promise.[24] Emphasizing client feedback, defining, measuring, and tracking performance, seeking continuous improvement, and encouraging worker participation can all promote better performance. Just as important, these features of TQM can support the other performance improvement initiatives that must be part of a genuine movement to improve government performance.

> **OMB should promote the adaptation of total quality management within the federal government by emphasizing client feedback, performance measurement, continuous improvement, and worker participation.**

6

Streamlining the Bureaucracy

IF THE PROGRESSIVES were partly wrong about some ideas, they were unquestionably right about one thing: institutional arrangements do matter. Increasing the number of bureaucratic layers lightens the supervisor's load by lessening the span of control, the number of subordinates who must be supervised. But more layers increase the distance from the top to the bottom of the hierarchy. As the distance increases, so does the potential severity of information loss. Orders from the top get muddled on the way down; reports from the bottom get lost or distorted on their way up.

Improving Middle Management

Modern information-processing technology makes the traditional organizational solution to the span-of-control problem—layering to provide intermediate points of control, middle managers who pass information up the chain and orders down to subordinates—less important. Senior managers are discovering that they can use management information systems instead of pyramids of fact finders to acquire and transmit information. Throughout the private sector, computerized networks have permitted corporations to slim down by eliminating middle-management slots. Our earlier recommendation that the federal government begin immediately to install an improved management information system has an important benefit: it can help the government reduce the layers in its hierarchy, redesign its middle-management function, and get closer to citizens. Thus

Congress should mandate that the OMB's deputy director for management, acting in concert with the director of OPM, formulate a plan to reduce at least one layer of management between the branch level and the assistant secretary or commissioner level in all federal executive departments, noncabinet executive branch agencies, and independent commissions.

Excess layers insulate top managers from good intelligence about what is happening at the front at the same time that they shield officials on the front from top-level policy surveillance and direction. Middle managers are most responsible for stripping away this insulation and making organizational communication work. Many federal middle managers, however, were hired as technical experts, not as managers. That, of course, is in accord with the original Progressive idea of the civil service, of hiring individuals based on technical knowledge. Now, however, many middle managers find themselves with important responsibilities for which they have inadequate training. Inadequate training has become even more a problem because in the realities of deficit politics training programs are often the first ones cut. Nevertheless, improving the government's middle management, both by developing a better administrative structure and by equipping managers with the skills they need, is a precondition for ensuring that performance reforms at the top are carried through to the bottom of the bureaucracy.

Each cabinet secretary, as well as the heads of noncabinet executive-branch agencies and inde-

**pendent commissions, should devise a strategy
for selecting prime candidates for management
positions and training them for the managerial
jobs they must perform.**

Because such career development requires modest funds,

**Congress should put high priority on appropriat-
ing money for these programs.**

Reducing the Number of Midlevel Political Appointees

Constant turnover at the top and close to the top of the federal personnel structure robs agencies of continuity and subjects the career work force to enormous uncertainty. Politically appointed superiors move through the revolving door, often with long lapses between the exit of one official and the confirmation of a replacement. The case for appointment flexibility, notwithstanding the problems of personnel turnover, is compelling for high policymaking positions such as cabinet secretaries, deputy secretaries, and assistant secretaries. There is no reason, however, why many of the billets occupied by lower-level quasi-political appointees—schedule C's—should not be converted to slots for career members of the senior executive service.

The total number of federal political appointees, some 3,000, including senior schedule C's, eliminates advancement opportunities for the very best careerists, often encouraging them to leave government just as they reach the top of their abilities. The number of political appointees has steadily increased over the years, even though the size of the total federal civilian work force has held steady since the early 1950s. The Volcker commission argued that the federal government needs no more than 2,000 political appointees.

**Congress should reduce the number of political
appointments in the federal bureaucracy by one-**

third, focusing especially on reducing the number of schedule C slots.

Consolidating Anachronistic Field Systems

Many federal agencies work with anachronistic field systems that date from the days before high-speed highways, sophisticated telecommunications, or computers. Under congressional pressure, the Department of Agriculture continues work through 11,000 field offices, many of which date from the 1930s. Some, indeed, date from the years immediately following the passage of the Smith-Levering Act in 1914. An America with many more farmers and less sophisticated communications needed a large field system. But the system is poorly fitted to today's rural problems. The General Accounting Office estimates that consolidating the department's field offices could produce annual savings of more than $100 million.[25]

USDA is an obvious case and one much discussed by federal bureaucracy watchers. A Washington joke has a weeping USDA employee answer, when asked why she is crying, "My farmer died!" But managers in all major agencies need to think carefully about how the agencies are organized and whether streamlined structures could enable managers to reduce costs and improve service. The Customs Service, the Department of Veterans Affairs, the Defense Department, and the Energy Department all have field systems developed to solve old problems. It is past time to bring these structures into line with actual functions. It is time, moreover, to improve the federal government's ability to offer one-stop shopping: locating related offices in the same facility so people do not have to spend time tracking federal agencies from town to town, office building to office building, to solve their problems.

Despite the economic and organizational logic, closing field offices is never easy. They provide jobs for workers and ready access for citizens. Not surprisingly, members of

Congress fight vigorously to protect the offices in their districts, just as they do to save defense installations. The commission to close defense bases provides a model to make the needed changes in the organization of domestic field offices.

A federal field office consolidation commission, patterned on the commission to close defense bases, should prepare a plan for consolidating or closing field offices across the federal bureaucracy.

Reinstating the President's Reorganization Authority

The president has intermittently held authority to reorganize the executive branch and rearrange personnel allotments. Congress has understandably been reluctant to yield too much power over the shape of the federal bureaucracy; the how of structure and personnel often determines the what of policy. The tug of war that has resulted, though, has robbed the president of flexibility to adapt the bureaucracy to today's problems. To resize the federal bureaucracy, the president needs the authority to reorganize quickly and decisively.

Congress should restore the president's statutory authority, which lapsed under the Reorganization Act of 1984, to restructure the federal bureaucracy, subject to congressional approval.

Coping at the Boundaries

To many citizens government seems vast, fragmented, and unresponsive, with programs directed to the narrow, self-contained interests of turf-battling agencies. The boundaries among government programs and the agencies that control them represent the problem of managing for results and serving the customer.

Organizational structures matter not only because of informational problems but also because of the boundaries they create. Federal managers often are unable to break through the compartmentalization of the government. But bureaucratic problems increasingly require solutions that cut across boundaries. Few important problems can be solved from within any single federal agency. As political scientist Hugh Heclo wrote, "If governance results from the joint interaction of many different parts . . . [the] appropriate unit of analysis is the cluster of interrelated parts that produces the results by which we are governed."[26] It is boundaries that create—and separate—the parts. The critical questions are which boundaries matter and why? What can be done to minimize problems and promote success?

Five kinds of boundaries are of concern: intersectoral (the distinction between public and private sectors, already discussed), interlevel (federal-state-local), interagency (for example, the kind of USDA-Interior-HHS-HUD coordination assumed by any integrated approach to the problem of rural poverty), interprogram (exemplified by conflicts within the field of pollution control—clean air strategies that worsen water pollution or accelerate landfill exhaustion), and intercultural (clashes of culture among officials with technical and managerial, or staff and line, responsibilities even within a single agency or program).

How can managers solve the boundary problem? Serving citizens today means finding ways to cross jurisdictional boundaries, which requires a more determined effort at all levels of the federal bureaucracy to cultivate government managers who are boundary spanners, managers who reach out to find colleagues in other agencies with whom they can solve problems. The need is to find ways to span multiple and cross-cutting boundaries, thereby improving government performance and responsiveness, but without sacrificing the core values that lie behind government's very existence.

Some encouraging examples can be cited. President Clinton's rural development initiative, for example, spawned a Monday Management Group (MMG), comprising forty-five federal executives from nearly every agency with a stake in rural problems, which meets biweekly to identify issues and develop solutions. The group's basic goal is to break down the barriers that stand in the way of solving rural problems; its members are quintessential boundary spanners. The MMG has promoted rural development councils in the states, and one council helped resolve a problem with which the city of Halstead, Kansas, was struggling. City officials hoped to build a $9.4 million project to control a long-term flooding problem from the Little Arkansas River. The officials painstakingly assembled the financing, acquired the land, and let contracts. They were stopped, however, by conflicts about a historic site. A delay clause in the contract threatened to cost $4,000 a day, and there was a danger that state support for the project might disappear. The state rural development council intervened and called all of the parties involved for a conference. The council was able to resolve most of the problems, but council members ran against a sixty-day waiting period mandated by the National Historic Preservation Act; only thirty days remained until the contract delay clause would trigger the penalty. Working with the National Advisory Council for Historic Preservation and members of Congress representing the area, the state council was able to conclude the review within thirty days. The boundary-spanning role of the council saved Halstead $120,000 by beating the deadline, and the town was able to begin the project.[27] In a policy world that is increasingly interconnected, performance will be advanced by encouraging boundary spanning.

Such innovations, however, are lagging far behind the galloping pace of organizational change. Boundary spanning can be both unconventional and risky—this is not the behavior that employee development programs in most federal agencies normally encourage. Boundary spanning requires a dynamic conception of the policy function. It requires that citizens and other stakeholders work actively with government managers to define what ought to be done, structure how it ought to be done, and assess what has been done. Because it is so hard to fix program goals in ways that will permit outcomes to be measured in precise ways, it becomes even more important to create problem-solving processes that are acceptable and open to all comers, on all sides of every boundary, at every stage of policy formulation and implementation. In such a process, participants can incrementally define what is to be done and how to do it.

OMB, OPM, and top agency officials should promote problem solving through boundary spanning as the keystone of their executive training programs.

The Most Important Boundary of All

Notwithstanding the increasingly wholesale nature of federal functions, significant areas of direct service delivery remain. For this reason, the most important boundary of all is the final one—between the government and the ordinary citizen. This is the boundary across which the Social Security Administration acts when it mails checks to the retired or disabled, across which the IRS acts when its agents answer telephone inquiries (usually correctly, but still with much too high an error rate), and across which the USDA acts when its Soil Stabilization and Conservation Service agents meet with local farmers to process their applications for inclusion in acreage-limitation programs. The list goes on and on.

Many federal programs touch large numbers of citizens but do so in ways that have earned them reputations for cumbersome or unresponsive administration, excessive complexity, or even rudeness. Red tape has generated fear and loathing of bureaucracy throughout the body politic.

At the most basic level of service delivery, the problem of bureaucratic complexity can be a forbidding tangle of regulatory requirements and confused or contradictory mandates from several agencies with simultaneous jurisdiction over artificially fragmented problem areas. To the ordinary citizen, therefore, improving government performance has less to do with inside-the-beltway reforms of civil service rules or procurement procedures than with cutting the red tape with which they must struggle.

Consider the person trying to start a small business and confronting the tax requirements, OSHA requirements, ERISA requirements, and others (in addition to the state and local requirements) that a new entrepreneur must meet. These requirements deter private entrepreneurship across the United States. (How many contributors to the design of EPA, OSHA, SSI, unemployment funding, immigration control programs, and the like have ever actually tried to start a small business and work through the procedures necessary for full compliance?)

OMB should launch a major effort to coordinate, consolidate, and make more user friendly the programs through which citizens directly encounter the federal government.

OMB's deputy director for management should organize several interdepartmental teams to troubleshoot and expedite, within a six-month period, a set of directly delivered federal programs.

7

Deregulating the Civil Service

LET ALL ELSE THAT troubles the public service be fixed—let a better balance be found between the public and private sectors, with all the needed improvements in procurement and policy management capabilities; let boundaries be spanned to achieve more coherent policies and simpler, integrated implementation regimes. Still, as long as rules of impenetrable complexity governing personnel recruitment, advancement, and job assignment and performance standards remain in place, the most dedicated and imaginative government employees could fail in the frustration of overregulation.

The civil service system is the crux of government's most enduring performance problems. There is a need to reduce or, where possible, eliminate personnel rules and work regulations that sap public employees' productivity, making careers in public service unattractive to talented, energetic potential candidates. There is a need to recognize the costs of excessive paperwork, of requirements to secure multiple approvals for routine decisions, of government jobs whose incumbents do little but monitor what is done by the incumbents of other government jobs.

Of course, many of these laws, rules, and surveillance procedures exist to prevent organized interests from unfairly penetrating the governance process and tenured civil servants from following their will instead of the public's. Indeed, protecting government from these dangers was what led to the creation of the civil service system more than a century ago. But bureaucratic constraints can also have perverse effects. Procedures that have been designed to check abuses by exhaustively monitoring workers breed discouragement and indifference. Given a workplace so uncongenial to the exercise of initiative, can we be surprised if bureaucrats sometimes lapse into inertia? Can we expect any basic or enduring change in the bureaucratic culture if the factors that explain the existence of that culture remain untouched by the reform movement?

In a 1987 article that attracted widespread attention, Constance Horner, director of the Office of Personnel Management, put the case for civil service deregulation:

> The size of the government work force could be substantially reduced if public managers had more flexibility in making basic personnel and purchasing decisions, and if lower paperwork requirements freed them to focus more on the services they are supposed to provide. [There are] tens of thousands of pages of regulations restricting their every move.
>
> Federal managers have little discretion to use pay to reward and retain good employees. As a rule, superior performance goes unrewarded with better pay. Nor does promotion come more swiftly to workers who show superior commitment and talent. Status on the basis of seniority is the dominant ethos of civil service administration. . . . It would be much better if senior managers could get their appropriated budgets and decide how many people to hire, at what pay levels, to get the job done.[28]

The move to deregulate the public service originates in important anomalies. One is the worsening fit between the federal personnel system, and the skills it attracts, and the actual functions performed by government. Another is the encrustation of rules that inhibit flexibility at a time government needs to display increasing agility. The key requirement of improving government performance should be to identify—and relax or even eliminate—rules that paralyze governance by immobilizing financial, human, and perhaps in some cases physical resources. Within agencies, these rules give managers little flexibility in encouraging high-performing employees. It would be neither feasible nor desirable to abolish the civil service general schedule, but there is no reason why a more loosely structured personnel system cannot be adopted.

Needed is more flexibility to promote superior performers, demote or fire mediocre ones, and transfer workers among jobs within agencies.

We need to modernize the service for an era of proxy government and to reshape the personnel system in ways that facilitate attracting and retaining outstanding performers as well as eliminating nonperformers.

Modernizing the Service in an Era of Proxy Government

A side effect of the government's shift to an increasingly wholesale orientation is the mismatch between a federal work force recruited and promoted on the basis of civil service norms and its mission. This government by proxy means that a far smaller proportion of the federal work force is directly involved in delivering goods and services to citizens than was once the case. Federal employees instead supervise a vast network of contractors, state and local governments, and other agents—the retailers who actually deliver the programs that the federal government funds. Exceptions exist in such critical areas as air traffic control, the administration of criminal justice (including corrections), and social security entitlement processing, but most federal employees work on the wholesale side of government. This government by proxy has important implications for modernizing the civil service system.

First, because civil servants are often intermediaries in the programs they manage, high-performance governance may depend as much on the performance of proxies as on the capabilities of their federal monitors. Second and as a corollary, wholesaling distances many civil servants from the citizens who are the ultimate service recipients. Far more often than in the past, federal employees must focus their attention on their program partners, the proxies, rather than on the satisfaction of their ultimate customers. That displacement, even detachment, of concern can make it easy for federal managers to forget why the programs exist to begin with and incline the entire system toward the seemingly unresponsive attitude that some citizens have discerned.

Third, the current federal personnel system was designed to produce a mix of employees different from the one that most government-by-proxy programs require. Insufficient attention has been paid to identifying and attracting people with the needed skills, such as contract negotiating and auditing. Likewise, little attention has been paid to providing the kinds of in-service training that would extend the skills of the technical specialists whom the existing system often targets for recruitment into the ranks of middle and upper management. It is no easy task to test and recruit candidates who will prove both amenable to continuous learning and adaptable to an environment of indirect supervision. Designing such tests presents a key challenge to OPM's personnel planners.

Fourth, the current personnel system gives managers little flexibility. One can hardly expect a one-size-fits-all design to facilitate dealing with the substantial differences that separate the Department of Defense (which, with half of all federal civilian employees, is involved principally with procurement, personnel, and supply problems) from the Department of Agriculture (which has a vast network of field agents charged with assisting rural development).

Attracting and Keeping the Best

We cannot improve government performance without high-quality, well-motivated government employees. Yet finding and hiring good employees takes far too much of managers' time. Worse, retaining the best technicians, administrators, and managers is often extremely difficult. Ending government's brain drain and repairing the low esteem with which elected officials and citizens alike hold civil servants are among the biggest problems in public personnel administration. Ridding government of shirking and otherwise underperforming employees may seem more trouble than the effort in particular cases is worth.

The place to begin is at the beginning: recruitment must be improved. For most prospective government employees, the federal hiring process is simply impenetrable. Getting information about jobs, finding out how to apply, and winding through the maze of the application process discourages virtually all job seekers. Simplifying and automating the job announcement and application process would be an important first step. So, too, would reducing the personnel processing turnaround times.

Congress should authorize the personnel office of each federal agency to simplify and automate the process of advertising its job openings. It should grant greater hiring authority to the agencies and charge personnel officials with improving service to applicants.

Getting the best is difficult enough; keeping them is even harder. Rewarding outstanding performance (or for that matter, withholding benefits, including promotions, from nonperformers) is largely incompatible with the current civil service system. Experiments with TQM, team approaches to policy problems, decentralization and delegation to employees (empowerment), and customer-centered management have been hamstrung by civil service and statutory limits on managers' abilities to reward outstanding employees. Performance rewards are frequently tiny when they exist at all. Administrators are often dispirited by congressional restraints on pay, bonuses, promotion, travel opportunities, and even small items like office furniture. "They must think that working for the government is reward enough," said one senior government official.[29] Poor performers, on the other hand, can count on drifting up through the general schedule with regular salary increases.

Members of Congress have long been reluctant to fund performance bonuses, especially those designed into the senior executive service. SESers have viewed the cutback in bonuses as a breach of faith. The bonuses should be restored. To make performance rewards real for all federal employees, moreover,

> **Congress should extend the bonus system for outstanding workers to cover 5 percent of the sub-SES classified service payroll and permit SES-level managers to allocate such bonus funds on the basis of demonstrated, documented contributions by GS-1 through GS-15 employees to agency missions.**

Remaking the Office of Personnel Management

President Reagan's first OPM director, Donald Devine, enraged many when he argued that the government needed only competent employees, not the best. The doctrine drew attacks from supporters of traditional civil service values. The decade-long bitterness, a debate over values and standards as well as over institutional goals and methods, makes it more difficult than ever to determine what to do with OPM.

Since its establishment in 1883 as the institutional cornerstone of the Progressive edifice, the Civil Service Commission and then its successor agency, OPM, have had responsibility for protecting the management of government from political interference. OPM staff members have worked with dedication and determination in the service of the Progressive ideal: a politically neutral, merit-based civil service. Ironically, however, the pursuit of neutrality gradually produced today's complex procedures for hiring, training, promoting, transferring, and paying career government employees.

Today's reformers argue that the system hamstrings government managers and erodes creativity among line workers. Others remind the reformers that history and contemporary theoretical analyses of the bureaucratic form suggest caution. Given the issue networks that characterize the governance process, the power of self-interest as a human motivation (particularly in the kind of market-oriented society that the reinventers want to accentuate), and the persistence of interest penetration in the American political process, more flexibility and less oversight in the public service can invite corruption.

The answer does not rest in choosing between neo-Progressive caution and acceptance of the more radical reforms. Rather the solutions lie in an incremental move toward flexibility, decentralization, and deregulation guided by a consciously worked-out public personnel philosophy. The proponents of the human resources approach have broached the outlines of such a philosophy. The distinction between public personnel administration under the guiding philosophy of human resources management and the more traditional connotations of personnel policy is more than merely terminological. Traditional public personnel administration tends to be identified with the application of the rules and procedures of the civil service system. Proponents of human resources management contend that OPM's real job is not to administer personnel rules but to cultivate the kind of work force that the government needs.[30] Where would OPM fit into a scheme revised along the lines advocated by human resources management?

First and most important, OPM must remain the voice for professionalism within the federal government. Although no one truly believes that a reverence for politically neutral competence must guide government employment policy, there must be a strong voice within the executive branch that reminds top officials of the historical and unresolvable tensions between political responsiveness and administrative competence in American government. OPM has an important institutional role in articulating how these issues shape policy. That argues as well for keeping OPM within the Executive Office of the President but independent of archpolitical units such as OMB.

Second, although the Office of Personnel Management has begun granting the agencies more discretion, far more decentralizing needs to be done. OPM should set overall employment policy and monitor agencies' performance. The agencies themselves, however, should be far more free to shape their needs. If executive branch agencies are allowed more discretion in personnel decisions, OPM can retain an important residual role as definer of broad personnel policies. The agencies must receive broad guidance within which to shape their own policies.

Third, how well the agencies' performance matches these broad policies must be monitored. If OPM gives up responsibility for the day-to-day details of personnel policy, its role as monitor of personnel performance will become far more important.

Fourth, OPM must be the federal planner on personnel matters for the future. The coming decades promise huge demographic changes, with far more women and minorities in the government work force. Tomorrow's work force will be much more complicated to manage than today's. It will be more racially, ethnically, and sexually diverse. More two-income families will demand better coordination of benefits, more flexible work scheduling, and careful planning for child care. Rapid technological changes will require people who can adapt quickly and are lifelong learners. Federal career employment, moreover, will have to be competitive with the private employment market in terms of pay and working conditions. OPM must look to the future and help chart a way for the government to get there.

Congress should authorize OPM to revise the classification procedure and federal pay system to give operating agencies more authority to shape their own personnel procedures while giving OPM responsibility for setting broad policy and overseeing the agencies' performance.

8

Cultivating a Culture of Performance

LOOSENING THE TANGLE of personnel constraints will improve morale and encourage initiative within the federal service. Deregulation will not, however, resolve some problems that figure prominently in the contemporary critique of bureaucracy. Cultivating a culture of performance is crucial to making reform work, to disseminating its values throughout the bureaucracy.

Philip Selznick, in *Leadership in Administration*, commented that effective institutional leaders cultivate a shared view of the nature, rightness, and importance of the organization's principal tasks.[31] Employees will then follow the agenda of the organization and perform its critical tasks up to standards despite the contrary urgings of immediate self-interest and the closeness of supervision to which they are subjected.

Culture and Institutional Leadership

A performance-driven federal government would be staffed by managers and administrators imbued with a new entrepreneurial spirit. At a press conference on April 15, 1993, Vice President Gore announced that the aim of the National Performance Review is nothing less than a revolutionary change in the culture of the federal bureaucracy.

With a cultural transformation, thousands of innovative actions taken day-in, day-out by members of an energized, performance-oriented federal work force would add up to constructive change in the bureaucracy at large.

Organizational culture is more than just an academic buzzword.[32] When Admiral James Watkins took over as secretary of energy during the Bush administration, he discovered that a culture of production had led the department's managers to underemphasize environmental and safety problems. For a decade safety reviews had warned that the existing culture needed to be replaced. "Within even a large, properly structured organization," one committee warned DOE officials, "safety is a reflection of institutional commitment and capability. Leadership at the policy-making level is essential, and dedication to safety must permeate the Department of Energy."[33] Watkins found that changing the culture was far more difficult than he imagined. But by continually insisting that safety and environmental issues had to receive high priority, he began to instill new values into departmental employees.

Many members of the career civil service have lived through efforts to change government—planning-programming-budgeting, management by objectives, and zero-based budgeting, to name a few—that left few lasting effects. The public servants who are to be the targets of new performance improvement efforts are notoriously skeptical of each new administrative pansophism.

What matters is the ability of leaders to inspire, to infuse value. Where such leaders are lacking, as they often are, or where they run out of steam or leave, as they often do, merely calling for a transformation of the bureaucracy will not suffice. Cultural change requires steady ongoing leadership from the top. It also demands followers who are willing to suspend the disbelief with which they are likely to greet the cheerleaders' initial exhortations. Such leaders are in short supply; so are such followers, especially among seasoned federal bureaucrats.

Any acculturative process, moreover, is labor intensive, slow to show results (requiring repeated cycles of education, exhortation, and reinforcement), and specific to the institution in question. According to Selznick, what we observe in the actual functioning of a typical organization are two related systems: the *organization* is a formal structure of offices and roles engineered to achieve efficiency; the *institution* is a collection of different meanings and evolves within and around the organization, framing the values to which members of the organization commit themselves. Selznick's repeated use of terms such as *distinctive competence* and *uniquely adapted* underscored his belief that what is institutional is also specific to the organization. The flexible thought patterns of the organizational problem solver—never mind the personal skills needed to motivate those who must implement new solutions—cannot be manufactured to specification.

The point here is similar to the one made in connection with the need for procurement reforms, reforms in federal service delivery, and the budgetary reforms that would be enacted if Congress passes Senate bill 20 in the form proposed by Senator Roth: neither once-and-for-all nor one-size-fits-all approaches make sense. Experimentation and selectivity imply carefully designed efforts accompanied by energetic leadership. The focus, or rather the foci, of these efforts should be on changing or reinforcing the organizational cultures of a few carefully selected agencies in which prospects seem especially promising.

The president should institute a Federal Mission Workshop consisting of twenty-five senior managers, both political appointees and SESers, who head bureau-level units of the federal government to meet monthly with the president in a continuing project of cabinetlike visibility and seriousness of purpose to regenerate agency cultures that are both entrepreneurial and result oriented.

Risk Taking within the Federal Service

Such an entrepreneurial culture would foster a willingness among federal workers to solve problems and take risks instead of falling back on routines or standard operating procedures when, as many citizens view the matter, it is slavish fealty to those routines that perpetuates the worst problems of public bureaucracy. How can an aggressive problem-solving attitude by all federal employees, not just those in senior supervisory positions, be encouraged when the political system itself often chops off heads that stick out too far? Problem solving means prudent risk taking; it means experimenting, moving past current and tested procedures. But risk taking, even if prudent, brings with it occasional failure. And the press and elected officials alike have discovered that horror stories sell. Steady superior performances by ninety-nine officials will be ignored while the isolated gross dereliction draws attention.

Management by exception—identifying problems and working hard to solve them—is an important administrative principle. Focusing solely on the exceptions, especially to generate political heat, however, can destroy the incentive to try. Indeed, one of the strongest reasons for moving to a performance-driven government is to be able to balance the picture.

> **Elected officials, notably the president and members of Congress, must lead the campaign for improved government performance by resisting the temptation to pick on isolated horror stories for immediate gain at the expense of discouraging managers from solving problems and taking risks.**

Improving performance from the bottom up has to build from top-down leadership.

Rebuilding Public Trust and Confidence

An avalanche of horror stories in the past decade has undercut public confidence in the government's ability to perform. Many tales seemed simply outrageous: coffeemakers that cost $7,000, screwdrivers that cost $90, bolts that cost $17. Reporters have discovered federal employees whose jobs are to measure the rate at which ketchup flows. The public reaction to these reports is ever deeper cynicism and profound distrust of government.

Some tales are indeed examples of waste. But more often they are the product of overspecification, overregulation, and overlegislation, in part because of excessive caution by federal managers and in part because Congress sometimes gives them no choice. The extensive specifications for military fruitcake ensure that contractors will not sneak substandard ingredients into large orders. Other items cost more because they are not off the shelf but custom-fitted parts of fighter planes or other complex pieces of equipment. Yet other high-priced items are the product of a government accounting system that tries to simplify complex recordkeeping by evening out overhead costs across a wide range of goods. That results in relatively large overhead for inexpensive items such as hammers and relatively small overhead for expensive items such as missiles. The story behind these stories, however, rarely gets out. They undercut the government's image, agency managers try to control damage, and the public's suspicions are fed yet again.

The unfortunate fact is that the government has too often fueled such suspicions by telling partial truths, distorting the facts, or refusing to answer questions. In the name of national security the Department of Energy and its predecessors were not always honest about the government's nuclear weapons production. As a result, many citizens assume anything DOE says is a lie. Now DOE finds itself involved with waste storage and environmental cleanup problems that require public involvement. But public distrust is interfering with its ability to get the job done, and delays, cost increases, and even more distrust have too often been the result.

Efforts to improve government performance are inseparable from improving public perceptions of government. Many of the steps to improve government require energy, resources, and trust. All will be in short supply if the public and the officials it elects begin with cynicism. Securing trust requires consistent, honest, and open communication from government officials. It requires government managers to anticipate the way decisions or actions might be viewed and to explain them fully. It requires admitting citizens into a full partnership with government.[34] Defense Department officials, for example, need to understand what decisions, such as overpriced tools, the public might find offensive. They need to anticipate complaints and explain clearly why the decisions have been made as they have.

An aggressive strategy to reach out to the public is critical for rebuilding public trust. It will not immediately reverse the distrust spawned by the past few decades, but it will set the stage for rebuilding popular support. Following through on this promise requires in turn a profound change in the culture of federal bureaucracies. Such a change, as we have seen, must begin with leadership by top officials, continue with followership by agency employees, and throughout evince a commitment to a citizen-centered focus. Without such changes, efforts to improve performance are likely to founder and the cycle of distrust is likely to continue.

Conclusion

Two Deficit Problems—Budget and Performance

BREAKING THE CYCLE of distrust requires solving the nation's two deficit problems. One is the federal budget deficit, which has become the overriding reality of American politics. Since the 1992 presidential election, the debate has become not whether but how to reduce it. It is the monster behind every door, and it drives every policy decision. Public officials, of course, have always worried about federal spending. It is the terrible burden of the deficit and the choices it creates that is new.

The other deficit is the federal performance deficit. Citizens have steadily lost confidence in the federal government's ability to deliver efficient, responsive, high-quality services. Overpriced toilet seats, pages of regulations for buying fruitcakes, lazy government employees who cannot be fired—these are as much the problem of government as the budget deficit.

The history of these deficits is long and frustrating. Budget deficit cutters have often argued that nothing else is more important. They have assumed that performance issues are routine matters best solved by lower-level officials. Performance deficit cutters have often worked from high principle but have focused on the details to the exclusion of the big politics. These approaches have led to false choices: seeking to reduce the budget deficit without worrying about the follow-through in government performance, or seeking to improve performance without recognizing the overwhelming political reality of the budget deficit. Reforms have therefore often produced a dilemma. In a quest for relevance, some performance reformers have linked themselves to budget deficit cutters and then have found that the budget deficit swept performance issues off the agenda. In a quest for technical integrity, other performance reformers have struck a course independent of the budget reformers and have found little audience.

This dilemma, however, is a false one. The simple fact is that without substantial improvements in government performance today's deficit cuts will produce tomorrow's disappointments. For most Americans, the deficit is less an economic reality than a symbol of the government's ungovernability. Bringing the deficit down will help demonstrate that elected officials can govern, but such reassurance will evaporate if citizens do not sense that the performance of government has improved just as dramatically. Moreover, without fundamental improvement in public performance, new management problems will surely erode the foundation of fiscal stability that deficit cutters seek to build.

The analysis and recommendations we have offered suggest that fundamental improvement in the management of government can produce better performance and reduce inefficiency. Greater efficiency can reduce government's cost and help reduce the budget deficit. We do, however, offer this warning: performance improvements that are perceived simply as deficit-cutting strategies quickly lose their legitimacy and alienate their allies. Performance reforms that fail to connect with the realities of deficit politics fail to win political support. Government needs to be made leaner and smarter if its performance is to improve, its costs are to be reduced, and future efforts such as health reform are not to be undercut. It is easy in the struggle over the budget deficit to assume that management will take care of itself. It is equally easy to get lost in the lofty rhetoric of performance improvement and forget the political realities of the budget deficit.

Only by bridging the gap between the twin deficits can either goal be achieved. That bridge has to be built by improving public management.

Our bridge rests on two pillars. First, improved public management requires the political determination to make it work. To a far greater degree than often recognized, the government's administrative problems are the product of the political system. Inflexibility, overregulation, excessive paperwork, and micromanagement are often the direct result of decisions made by the Office of Management and Budget and Congress to micromanage the administrative system. Sometimes these problems come as a reflex to prevent past abuses from recurring. Sometimes they result from efforts to steer the distribution of contracts, control eligibility for entitlements, or shape other products of administration agencies. Sometimes they occur for largely symbolic reasons, such as the urge to reduce government paperwork and the number of regulations. Because much of the tangle impeding government efficiency comes from top officials of both the legislative and executive branches, it will require them to focus their political will if government management is to be improved. Improving performance requires Congress to become an active partner in federal management. Even more important, improved performance simply will not happen without strong and sustained presidential commitment. Progress will quickly erode without aggressive political leadership; management is not a detail that can become a secondary consideration or performance will suffer.

Government administration is encrusted with rules and procedures from an earlier time that are poorly matched to today's problems. Government finds itself choking on its own regulations and procedures. Even worse, its capacity to tackle new problems is weakened. Federal managers find themselves without the right skills, structure, or procedures to be effective partners with state and local governments, nonprofit organizations, and private contractors. Frequently they discover that their rules and policies get in the way. Quality results demand building the capacity to do the job. Improved government management will require the development of new tools better suited to today's problems.

Political micromanagement and the mismatch of government's tools with its problems have crippled public management, increased government inefficiency, and impeded performance. Perhaps worst of all, they have provoked a widespread distrust of the American system: by elected officials, who cannot understand why administrators do not produce better results; by administrators, who complain about constant interference by elected officials as they try to do their jobs; and by citizens, who curse elected officials and administrators for squabbling among themselves and for overlooking why they are there to begin with.

We have recommended building our bridge with these blocks:

—a personnel system that gives managers the flexibility to manage creatively;

—a budgetary system that matches resources to results;

—a procurement system that enables government to work more creatively with its private partners;

—fresh attention to federalism to invigorate the federal-state-local partnership;

—greater capacity to equip government to do its job responsively, effectively, and efficiently;

—administrative leadership that encourages managers to reach across the multiple boundaries of government to solve problems;

—political leadership from both the executive and legislative branches to enhance government administration and bridge the gulf between deficit politics and performance improvement.

Neither deficit can be solved quickly or easily. We can, however, make steady progress to put us on the way. We can also recognize that only by bridging both deficits with better public management can we solve either one.

Notes

1. David Osborne and Ted Gaebler, *Reinventing Government: How the Entrepreneurial Spirit Is Transforming the Public Sector* (Addison-Wesley, 1992).

2. Paul A. Volcker, *Leadership for America: Rebuilding the Public Service—The Report of the National Commission on the Public Service and the Task Force Reports to the National Commission on the Public Service* (National Commission on Public Service, 1989).

3. Grant McConnell, *Private Power and American Democracy* (Knopf, 1966), pp. 49–50.

4. To a lesser extent, the same is true of Hugh Heclo's concept of "issue networks." Heclo contends that parties with an interest in a given area of public policy develop informal relationships to help them stay in touch, trade information, debate policy proposals, and bring ideas to legislative hearings and agency rulemakings—generally to try to pressure that portion of the process that affects their industry, profession, or cause. See Hugh Heclo, "Issue Networks and the Executive Establishment," in Anthony King, ed., *The New American Political System* (Washington: American Enterprise Institute, 1978), pp. 102–05.

5. Kenneth Culp Davis, *Discretionary Justice: A Preliminary Inquiry* (University of Illinois Press, 1971), chap. 4.

6. See R. H. Coase, "The Nature of the Firm," *Economica*, vol. 4 (November 1937), pp. 386–405; and Oliver E. Williamson, *Markets and Hierarchies: Analysis and Antitrust Implications—A Study in the Economics of Internal Organization* (Free Press, 1975). See also Gerald Garvey, *Facing the Bureaucracy: Living and Dying in a Federal Agency* (San Francisco: Jossey-Bass, 1993).

7. The real cost of a traded item is its market price plus the transaction costs of the exchange (to which, strictly speaking, we must also

add any external costs of the product in question, such as the costs of any pollution that the makers of the product generate).

8. Woodrow Wilson, "The Study of Administration," *Political Science Quarterly*, vol. 2 (June 1887), reprinted in Richard J. Stillman II, ed., *Public Administration: Concepts and Cases*, 5th ed. (Houghton Mifflin, 1992), p. 14.

9. See Frederick W. Taylor, *The Principles of Scientific Management* (Norton, [1911] 1967), pp. 43–47, 137–38; and William R. Spriegel and Clark Myers, eds., *The Writings of the Gilbreths* (Homewood, Ill.: Irwin, 1953). See also Samuel Haber, *Efficiency and Uplift: Scientific Management in the Progressive Era, 1890–1920* (University of Chicago Press, 1964), chap. 3.

10. National Academy of Public Administration, *Leading People in Change: Empowerment, Commitment, Accountability* (Washington, April 1993), p. 36.

11. General Accounting Office, *Government Contractors: Are Service Contractors Performing Inherently Governmental Functions?* GAO/GGD-92-11 (November 1991).

12. See Donald F. Kettl, *Sharing Power: Public Governance and Private Markets* (Brookings, 1993).

13. Quoted in 58 Fed. Reg. 32109 (1993).

14. Kettl, *Sharing Power*, chap. 6.

15. See Steven Kelman, *Procurement and Public Management: The Fear of Discretion and the Quality of Government Performance* (Washington: AEI Press, 1990), p. 1. See also Kelman, "Deregulating Federal Procurement: Nothing to Fear But Discretion Itself?" in John J. DiIulio, Jr., ed., *Deregulating the Public Service: Can Government Be Improved?* (Brookings, forthcoming).

16. U.S. House of Representatives, Committee on Government Operations, *Managing the Federal Government: A Decade of Decline*, majority staff report (1992), p. 1.

17. Office of Management and Budget, *Budget Baselines, Historical Data, and Alternatives for the Future* (January 1993), pp. 195–232.

18. General Accounting Office, *Information Management and Technology Issues*, GAO/OCG-93-5TR (December 1992), pp. 19–21.

19. General Accounting Office, *Improving Government: Measuring Performance and Acting on Proposals for Change*, statement of Charles Bowsher, Comptroller General of the United States, GAO/T-GGD-93-14 (March 23, 1993), p. 3.

20. General Accounting Office, *Program Performance Measures: Federal Agency Collection and Use of Performance Data*, GAO/GGD-92-65 (May 1992), pp. 1–2.

21. H. George Frederickson, "Painting Bull's-Eyes around Bullet Holes," *Governing*, vol. 6 (October 1992), p. 13.

22. General Accounting Office, *Integrating Human Services: Linking At-Risk Families with Services More Successful Than System Reform Efforts*, GAO/HRD-92-108 (September 1992), esp. pp. 3–7.

23. General Accounting Office, *Quality Management: Survey of Federal Organizations*, GAO/GGD-93-9BR (October 1992), pp. 16–17.

24. James E. Swiss, "Adapting Total Quality Management (TQM) to Government," *Public Administration Review*, vol. 52 (July–August 1992), p. 360.

25. General Accounting Office, *Government Management Issues*, GAO/OCG-93-3TR (December 1992), pp. 38–39.

26. Hugh Heclo, "Comments," in Lester M. Salamon and Michael S. Lund, eds., *The Reagan Presidency and the Governing of America* (Washington: Urban Institute Press, 1984), p. 374.

27. National Rural Economic Development Institute, "Kansas Council Clears the Way for Rural Development Agency" (University of Wisconsin-Extension, Madison, February 1993).

28. Constance Horner, "Beyond Mr. Gradgrind," *Policy Review*, no. 44 (Spring 1988), pp. 34–35.

29. Interview with the authors.

30. See, for example, National Academy of Public Administration, *Leading People in Change*, esp. p. 33.

31. Philip Selznick, *Leadership in Administration: A Sociological Interpretation* (Row, Peterson, 1957), chap. 1.

32. John J. DiIulio, Jr., "Principled Agents: The Cultural Basis of Behavior in a Federal Government Bureaucracy," *Journal of Socioeconomics* (forthcoming).

33. Meserve Committee, *Safety Issues at the Defense Production Reactors: A Report to the U.S. Department of Energy* (Washington: National Academy Press, 1987), p. 83.

34. See, for example, Task Force on Radioactive Waste Management, Secretary of Energy Advisory Board, *Draft Final Report* (December 1992), esp. pp. 1–3.

Index

125140

Swiss, James E., 53

Taft commission, 7, 8, 47
Taylor, Frederick Winslow, 14, 24
Technology and information
    management, 42, 43, 44–46, 55
Timing of administrative reforms,
    9–10
Total quality management (TQM),
    11, 48, 49, 52–54, 68
Training of civil service employees,
    43, 56–57, 67
Transaction costs, 24–25
Transportation, U.S. Department of
    (DOT), 34

Trust, public, in government, 51,
    77–78

Veterans Affairs, U.S. Department
    of, 58
Volcker, Paul A., 4
Volcker commission, 4, 58

Watkins, James D., 74
Weber, Max, 14, 24
Wholesaling of federal services, 32,
    39, 66–67
Wilson, Woodrow, 14, 25
Winter, William F., 4
Work Projects Administration, 14

DATE DUE

HIGHSMITH 45-220